Real World

Colouring Book

For Advanced Users & Adults

50 Images

**Created From Real Life Photos
For You To Colour As You Please.**

ISBN 978-0-359-86332-7
90000
9 780359 863327

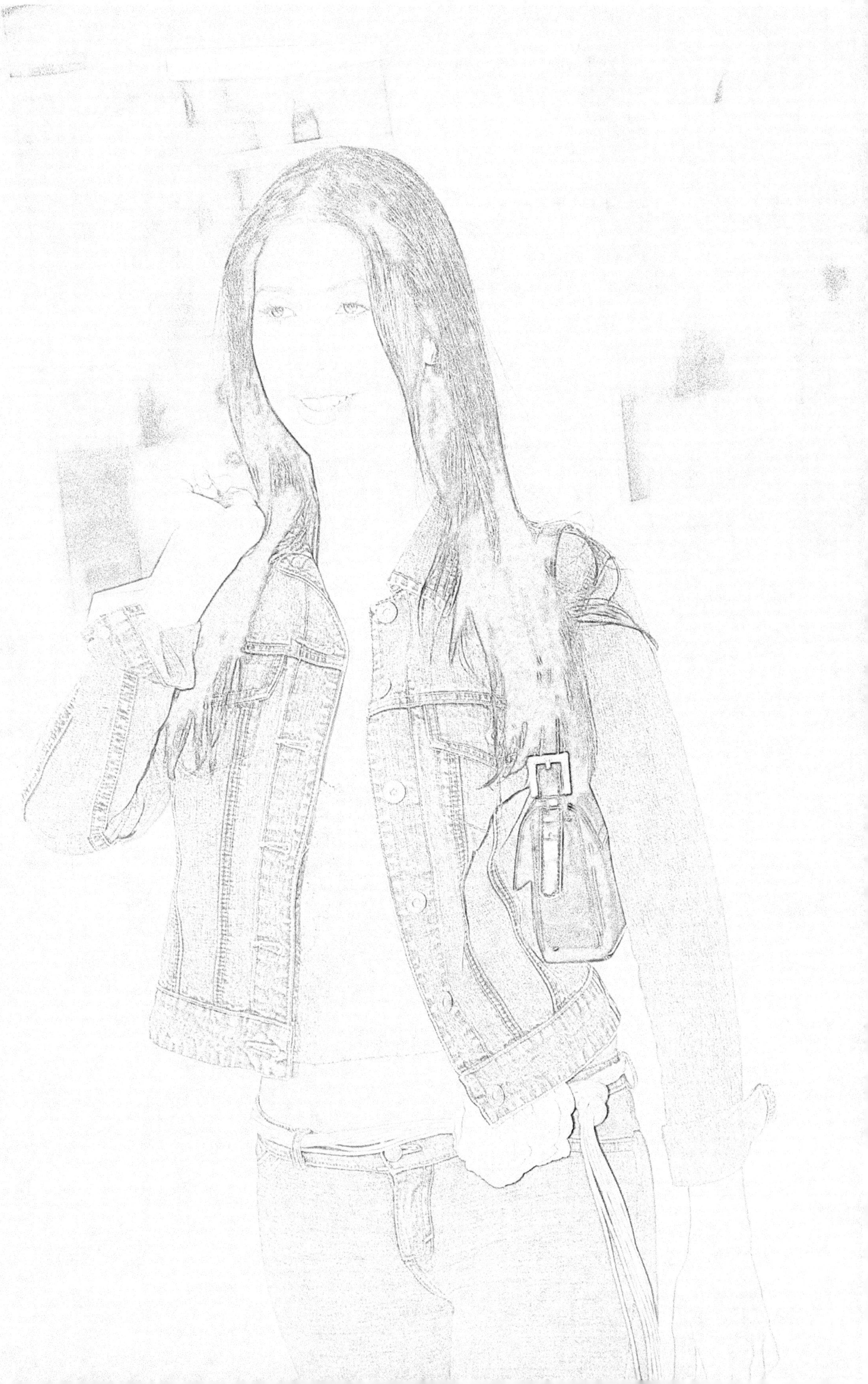

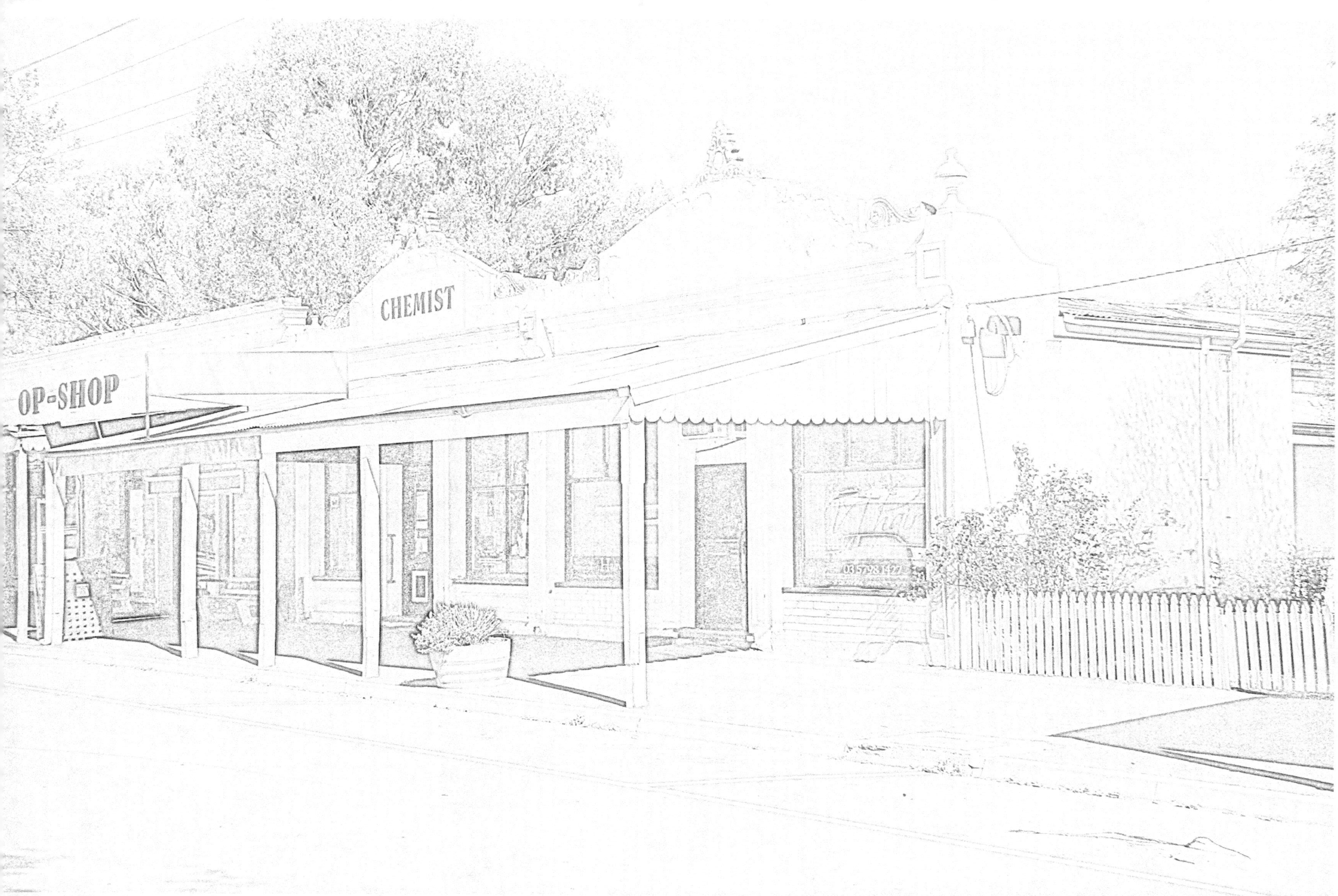
CHEMIST
OP-SHOP

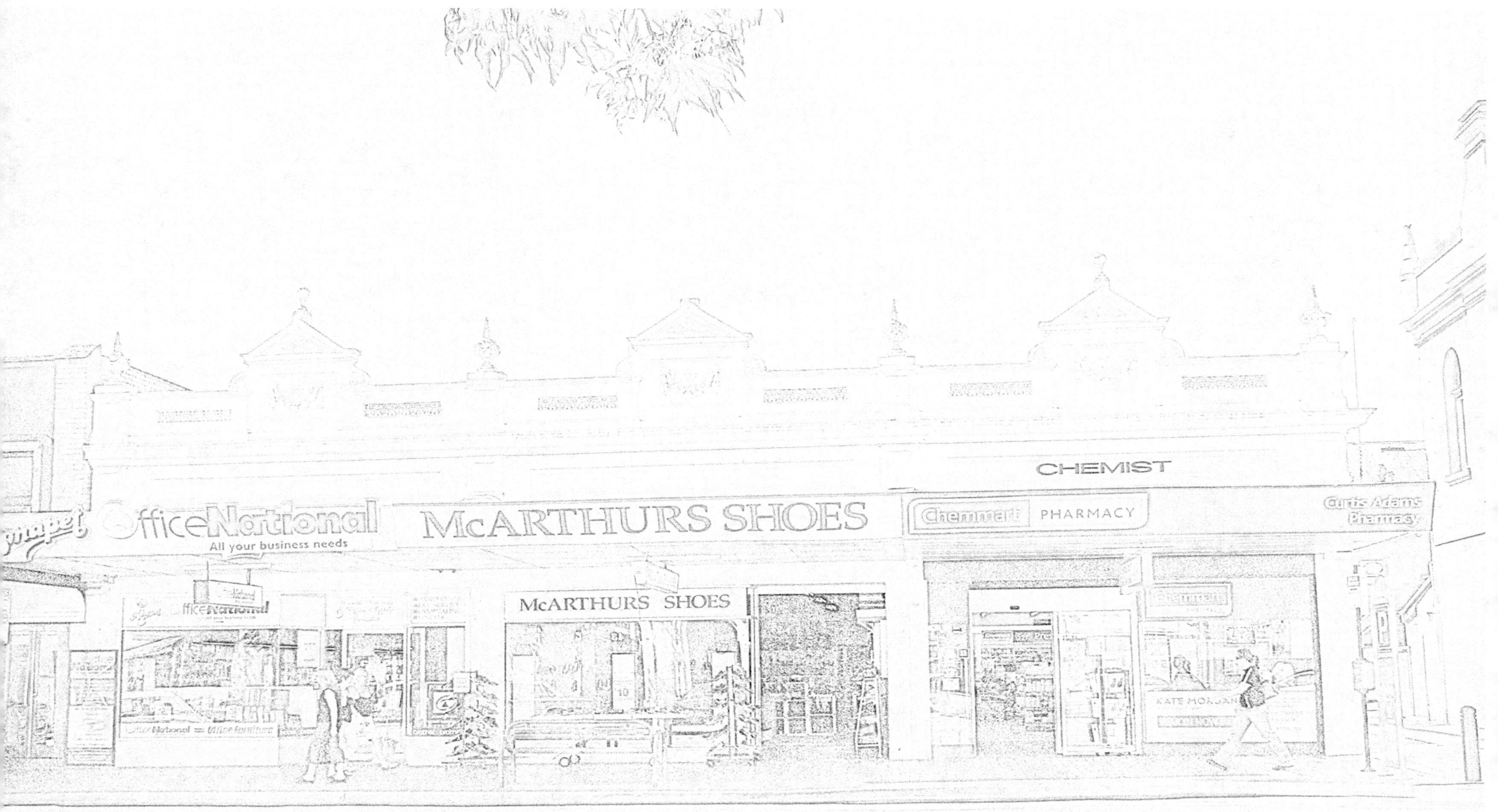
officeNational
All your business needs
McARTHURS SHOES
Chemmart PHARMACY
Curtis Adams Pharmacy
CHEMIST
McARTHURS SHOES
KATE MORGAN

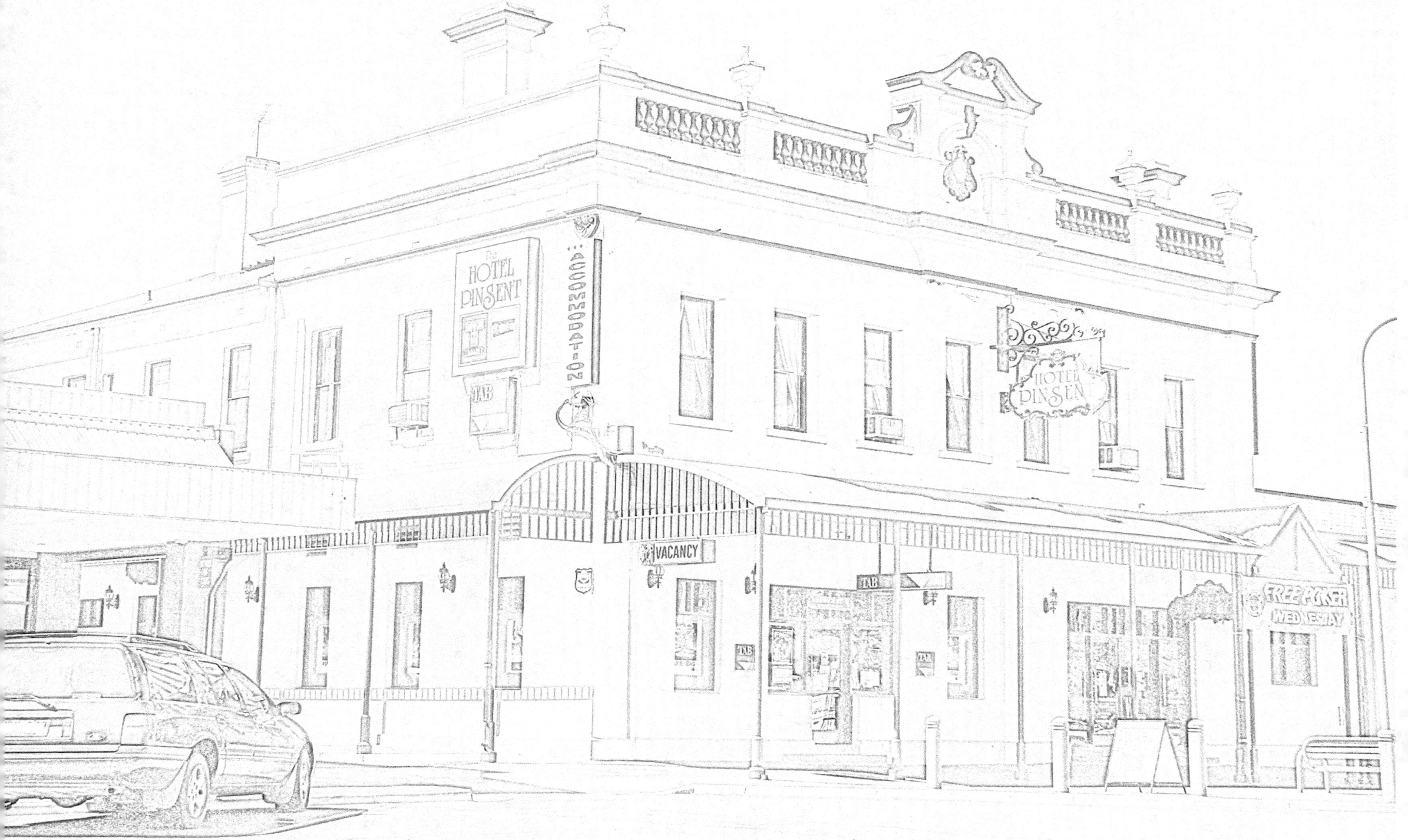
The
HOTEL
PINSENT
TAB
ACCOMMODATION
HOTEL
PINSENT
VACANCY
TAB
TAB
TAB
FREE POKER
WEDNESDAY

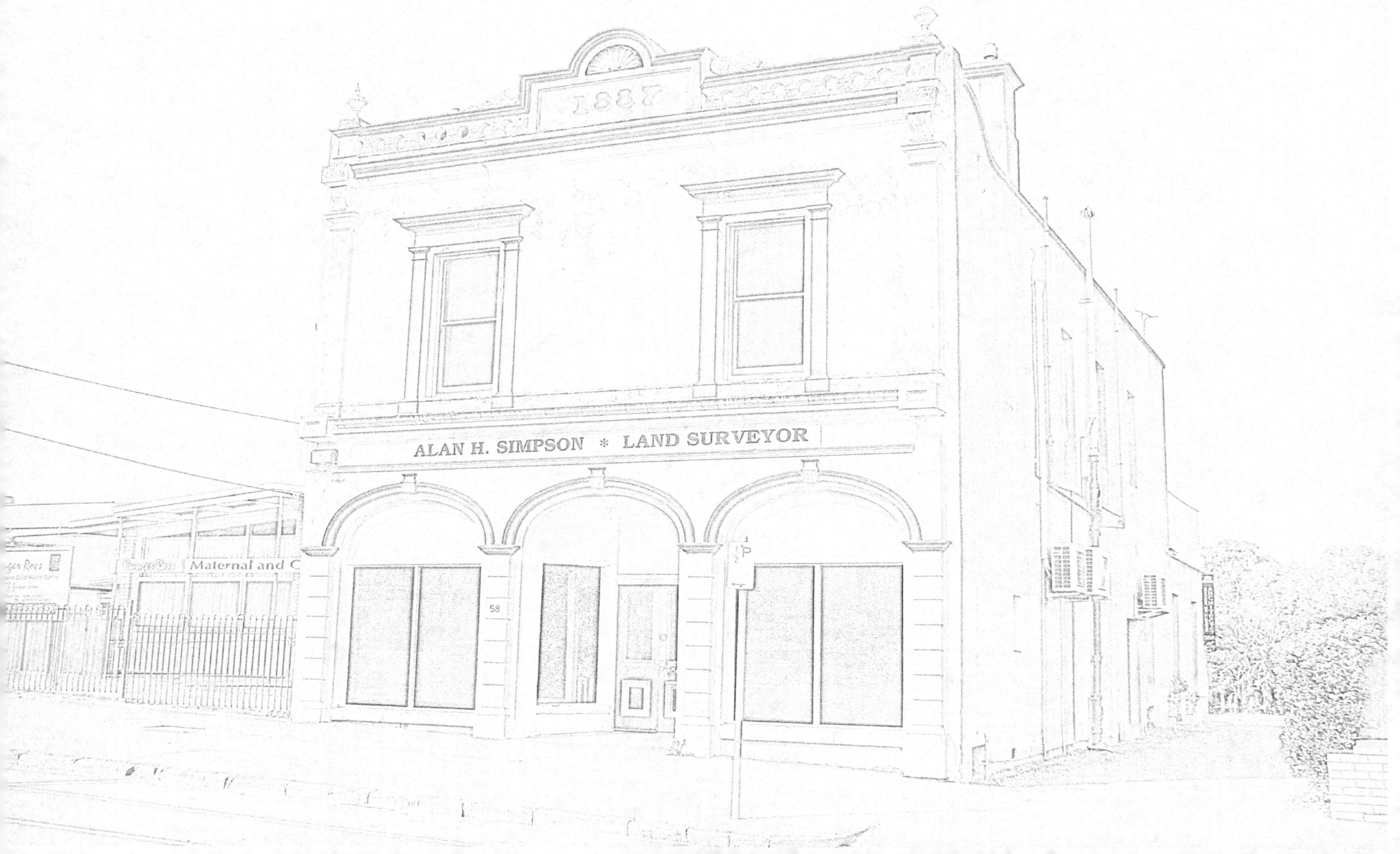
1887
ALAN H. SIMPSON * LAND SURVEYOR
58
Maternal and C

ESTD 1869
BUILDING
SOCIETY
86-88
PAJERO

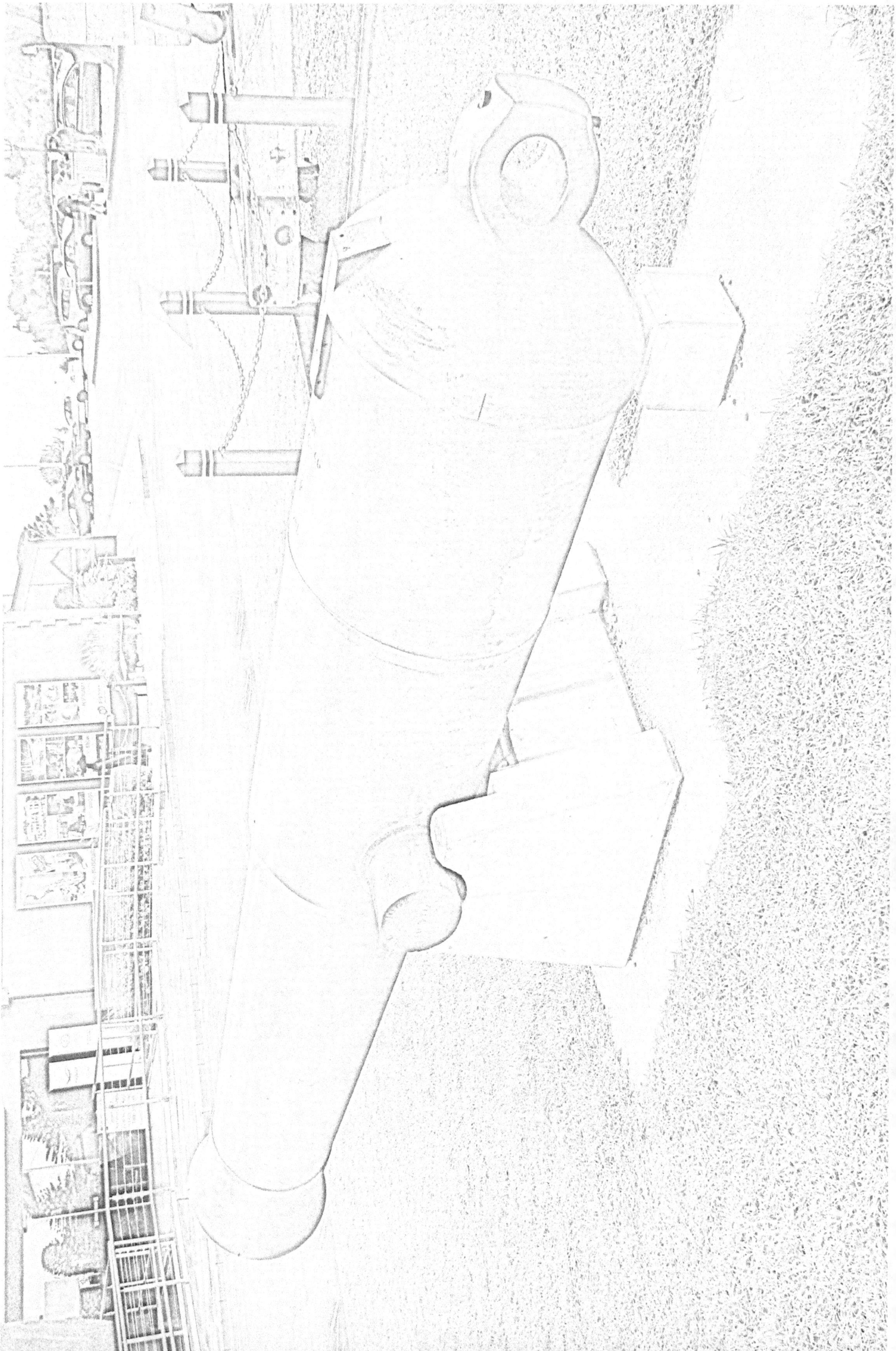

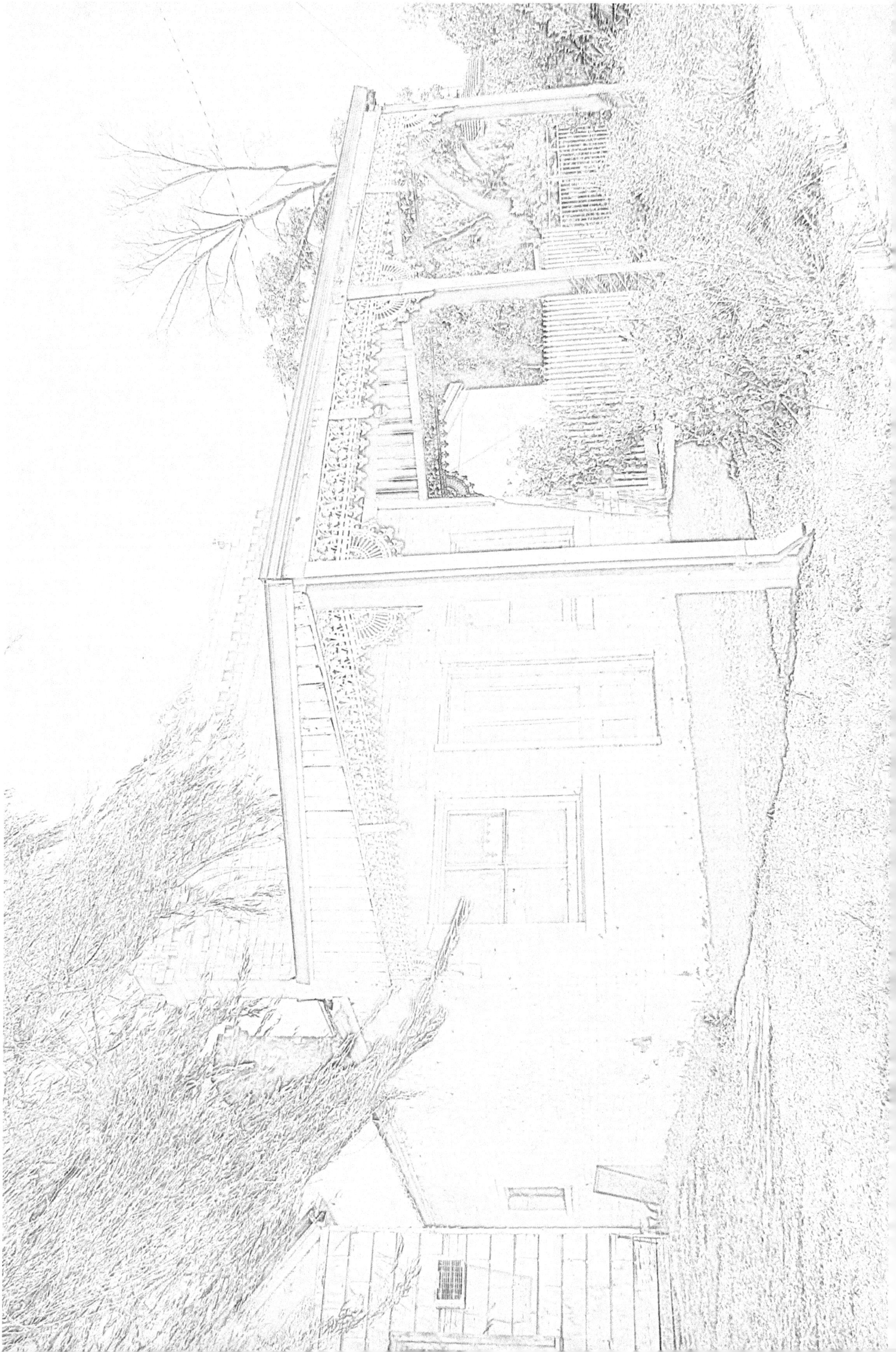

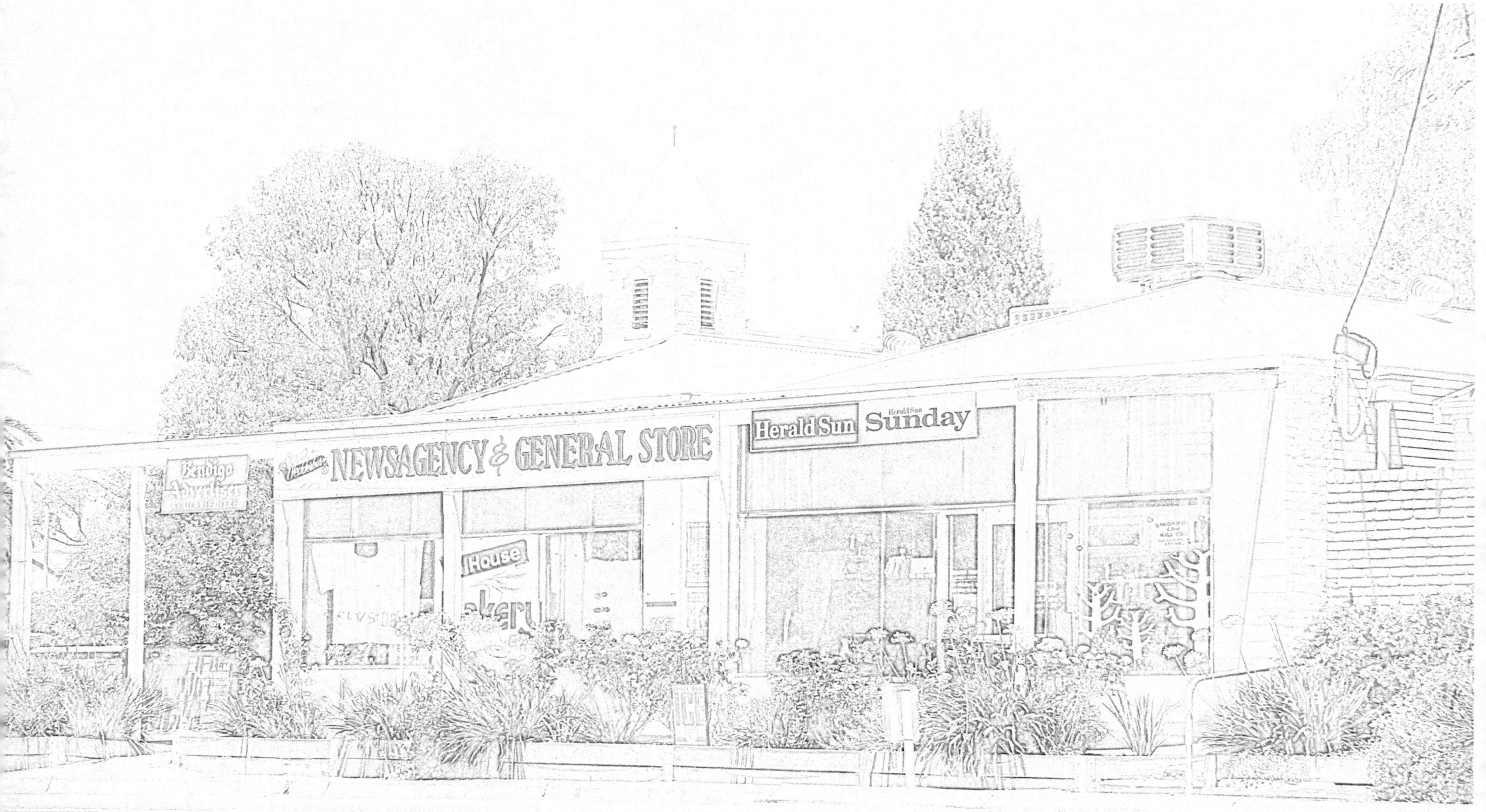
Bendigo Advertiser
NEWSAGENCY & GENERAL STORE
Herald Sun
Herald Sun Sunday
House

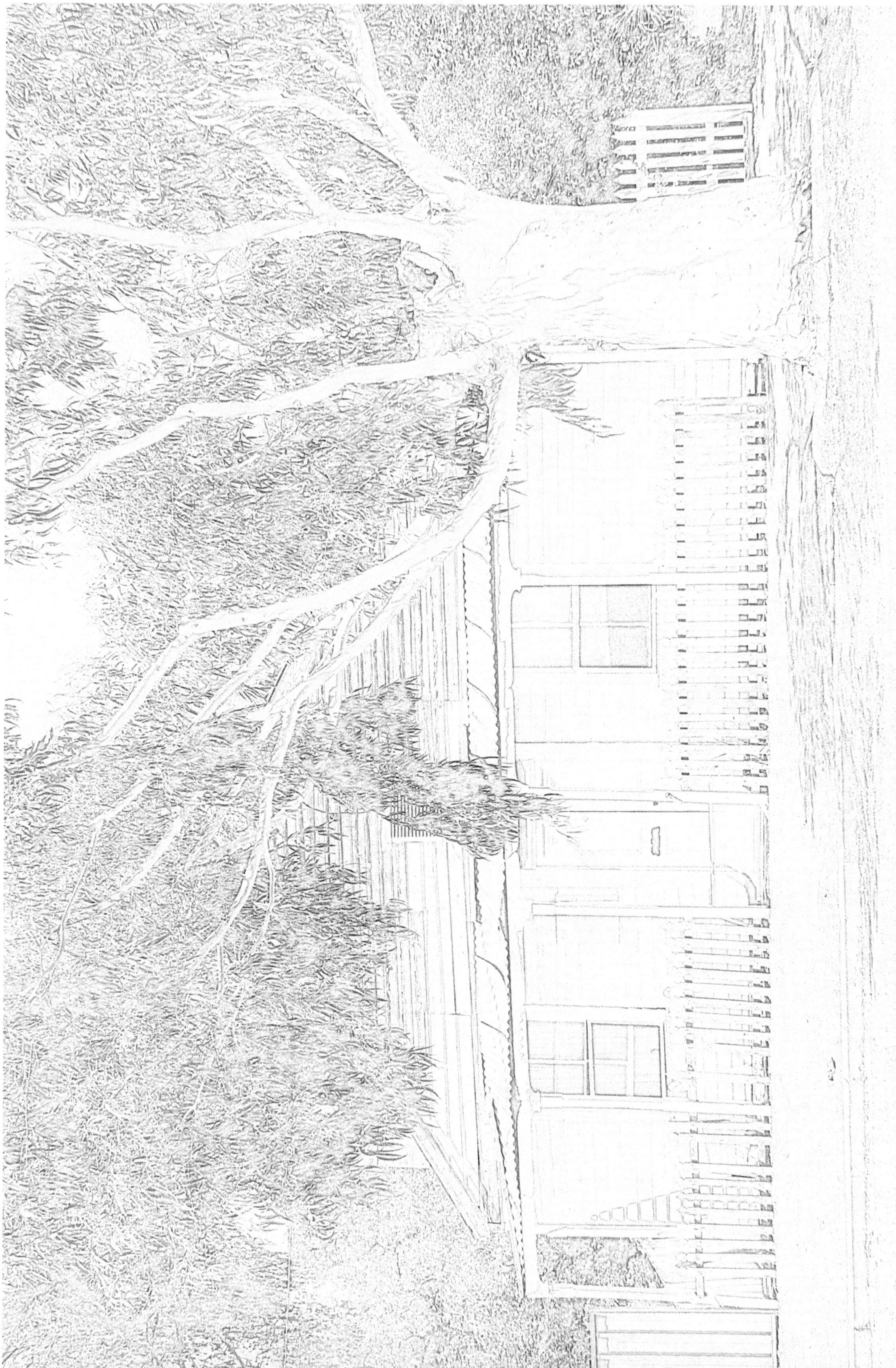

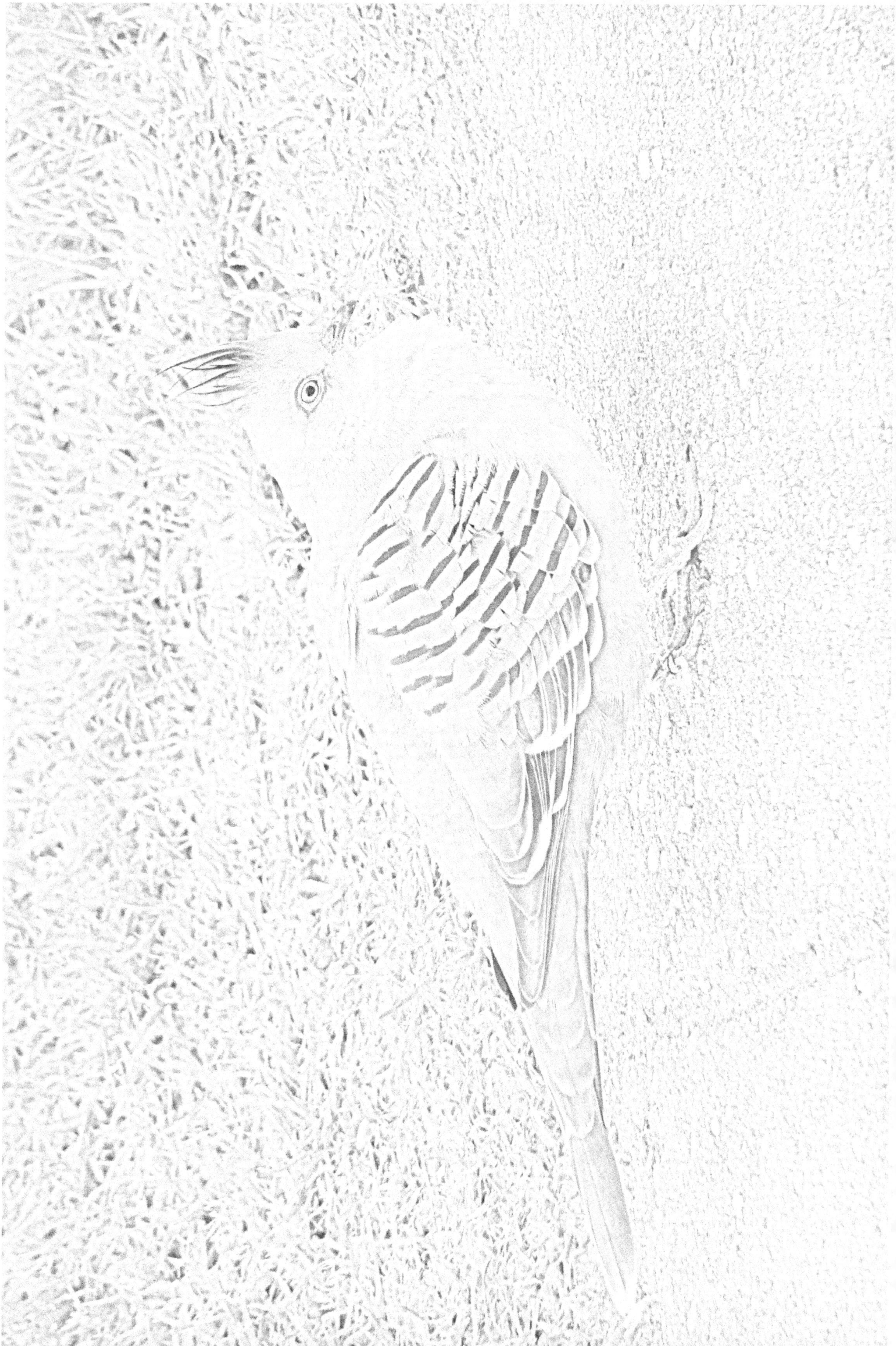

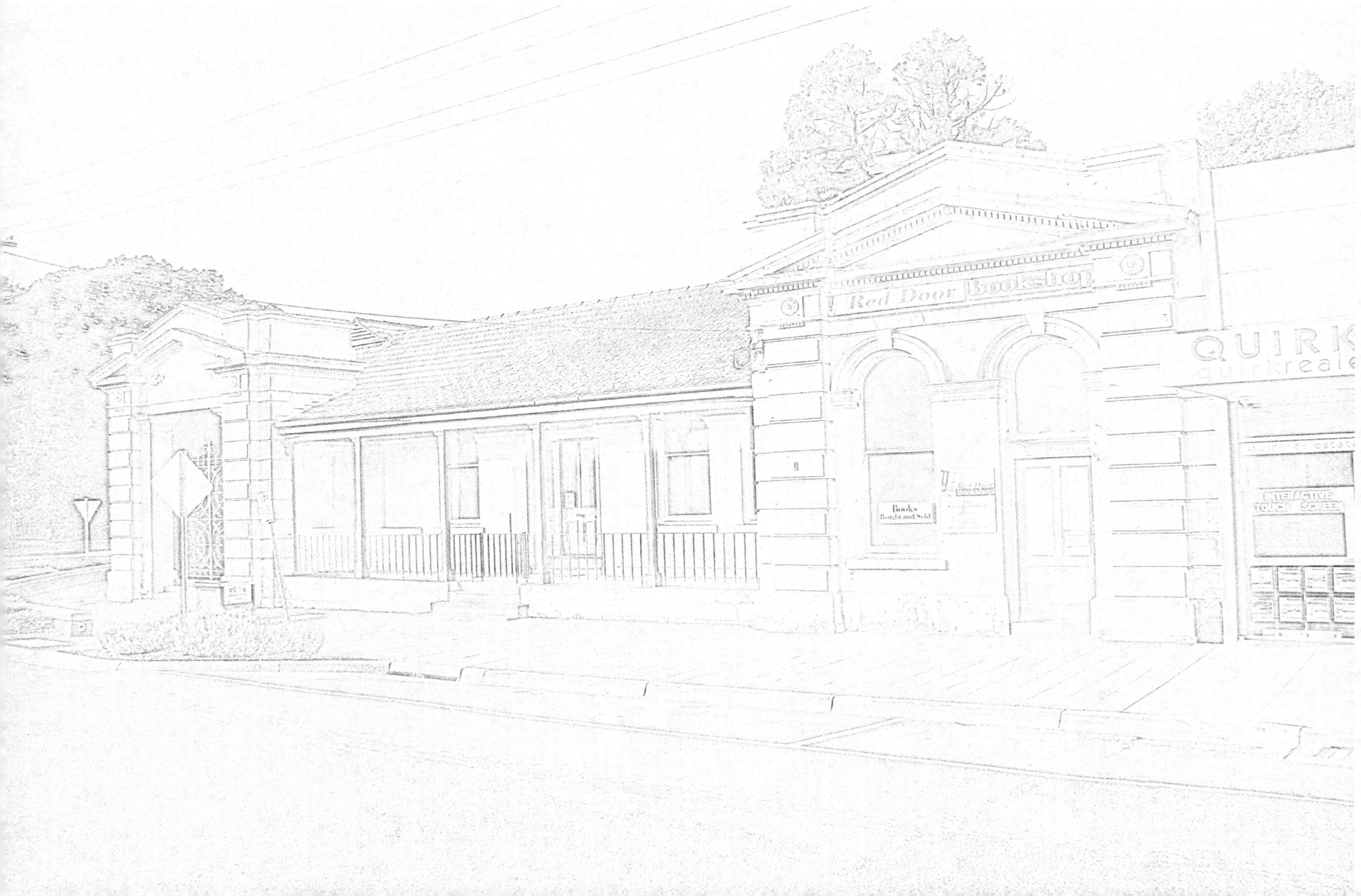
Red Door Bookshop
Books
Bought and Sold
QUIRK

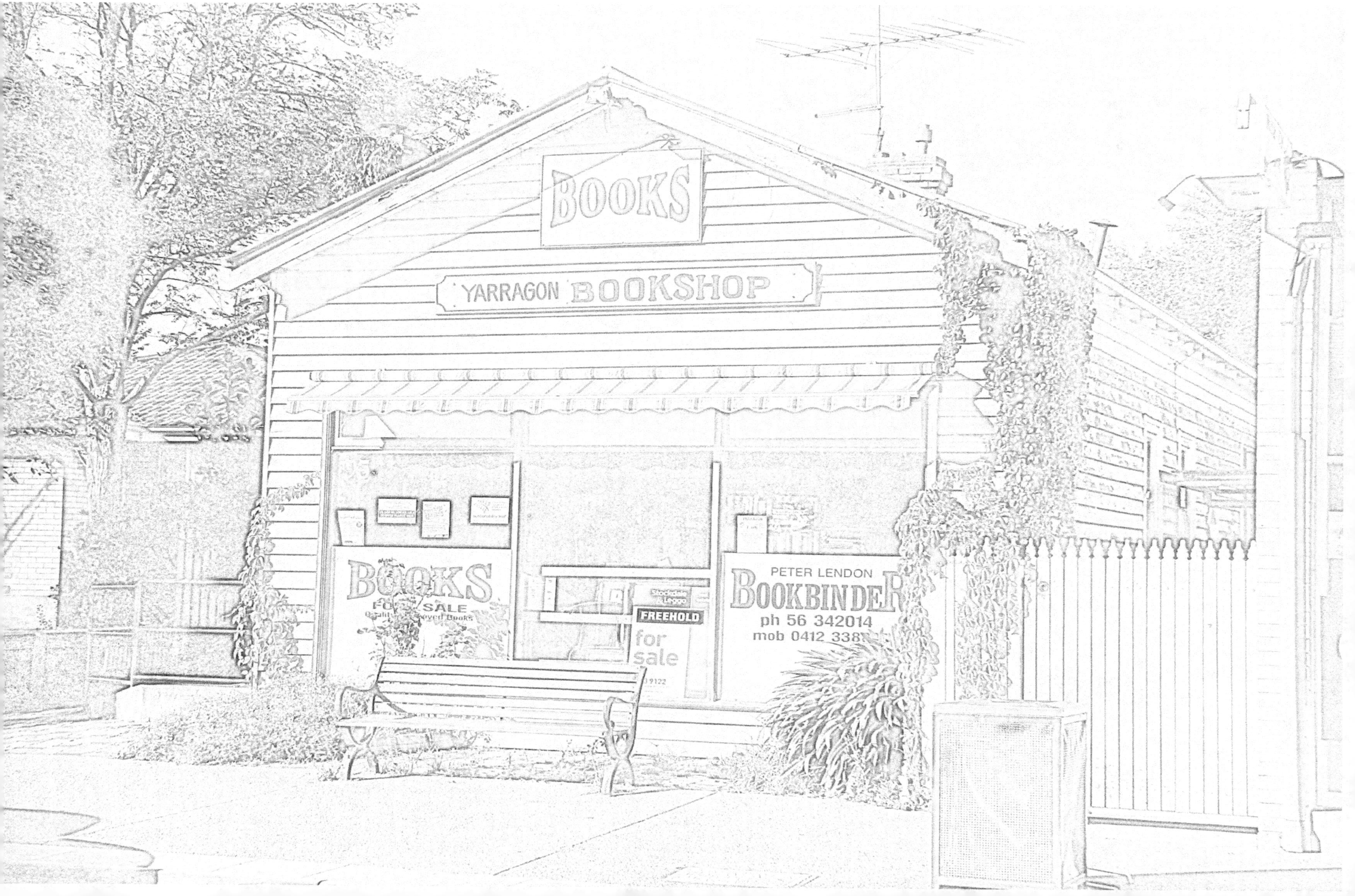
BOOKS
YARRAGON BOOKSHOP
BOOKS
FOR SALE
FREEHOLD
for sale
PETER LENDON
BOOKBINDER
ph 56 342014

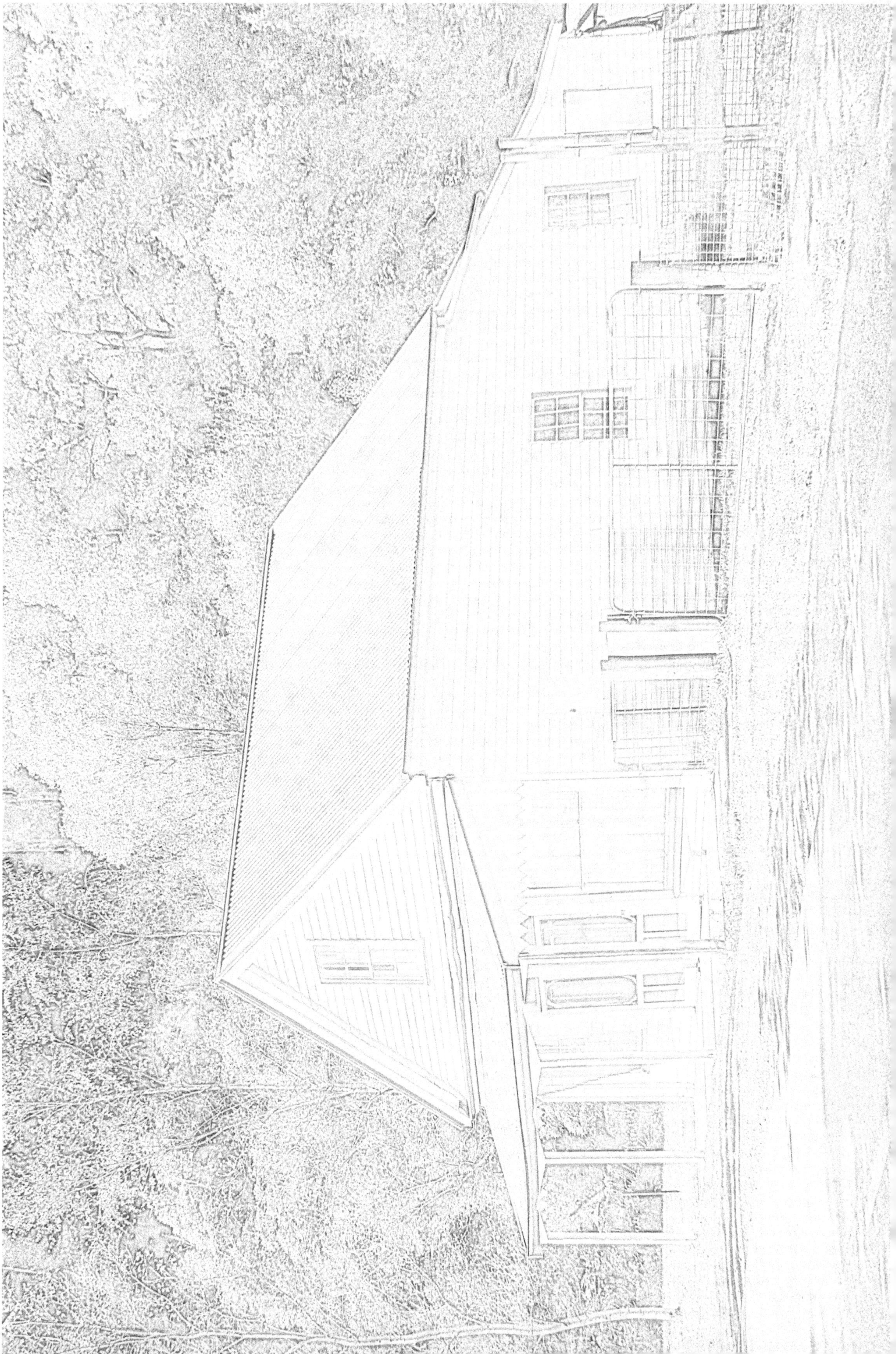

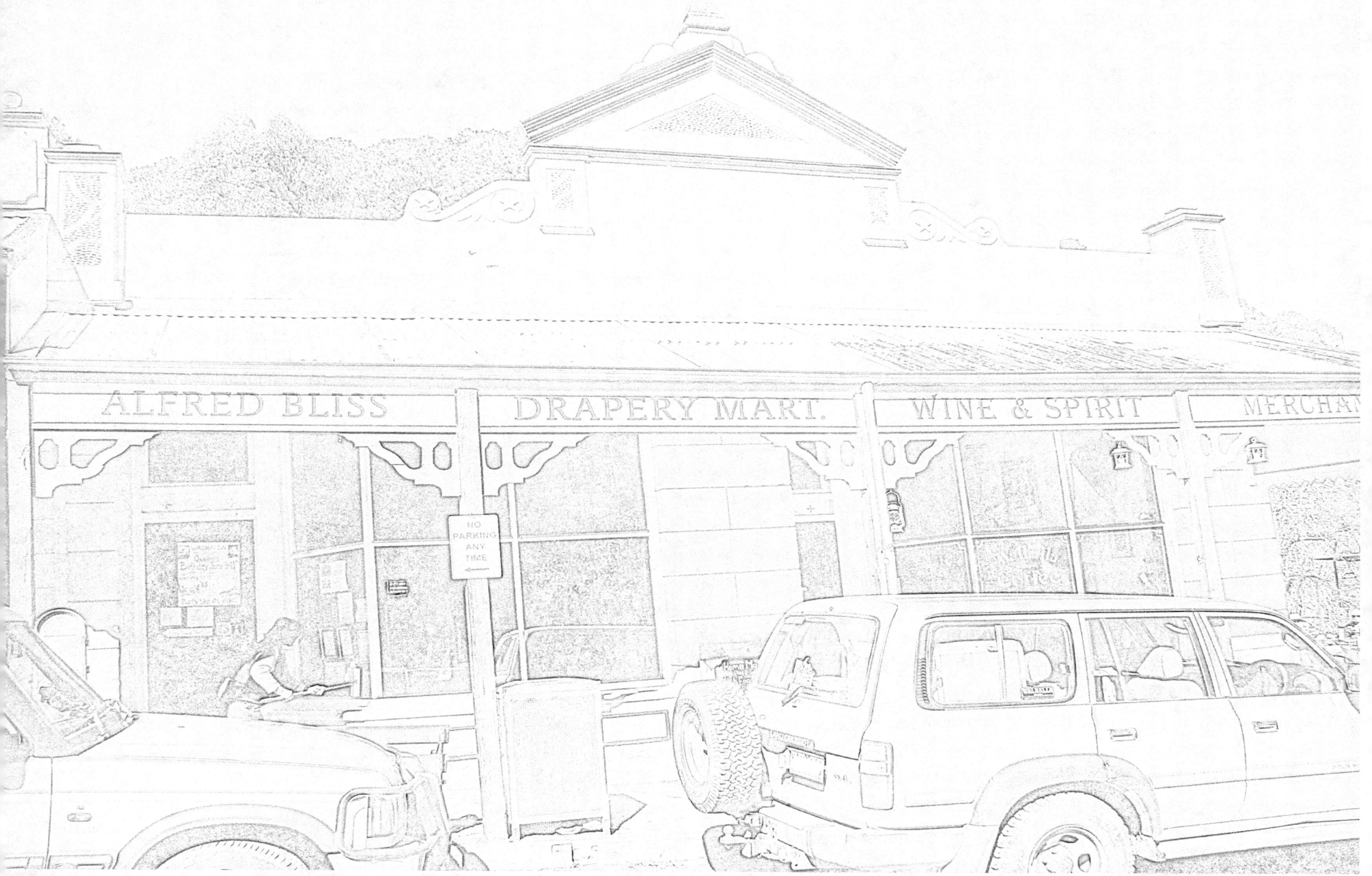
ALFRED BLISS
DRAPERY MART.
WINE & SPIRIT
NO PARKING ANY TIME

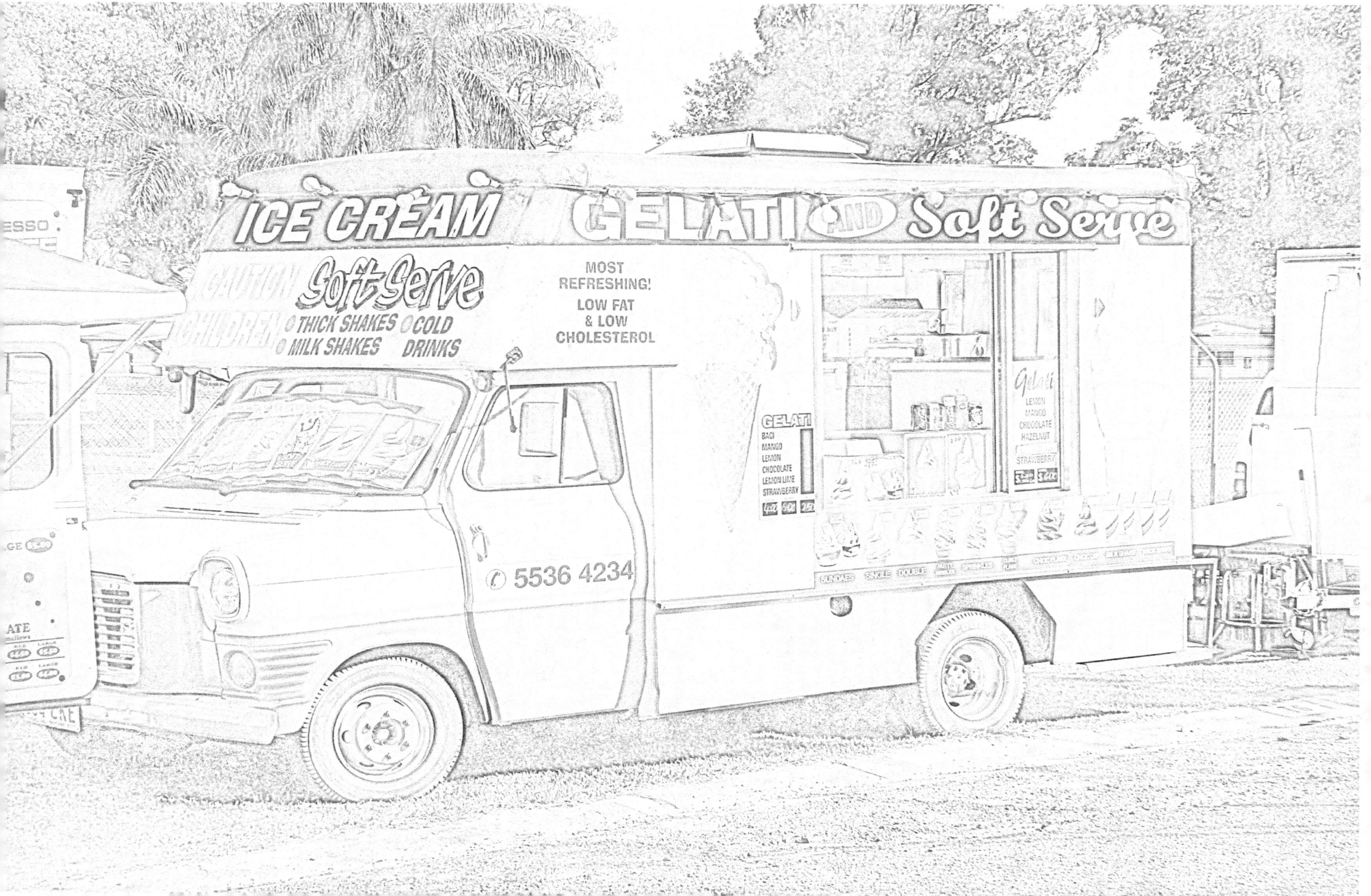
ICE CREAM
GELATI AND Soft Serve
CAUTION CHILDREN
Soft Serve
THICK SHAKES
MILK SHAKES
COLD DRINKS
MOST REFRESHING!
LOW FAT & LOW CHOLESTEROL
5536 4234
GELATI
BACI
MANGO
LEMON
CHOCOLATE
LEMON LIME
STRAWBERRY
Gelati
LEMON
MANGO
CHOCOLATE
HAZELNUT
STRAWBERRY
SUNDAES
SINGLE
DOUBLE

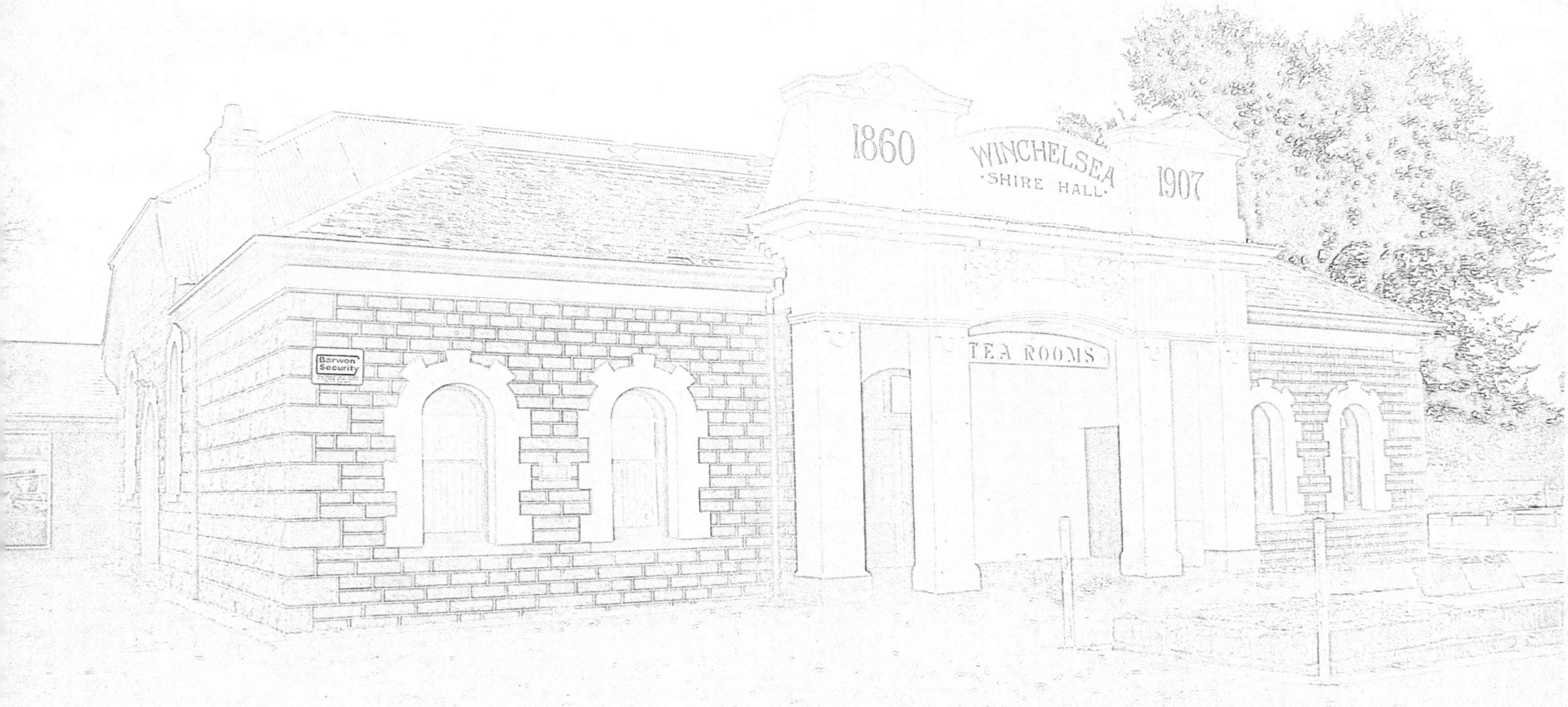
1860
WINCHELSEA
·SHIRE HALL·
1907
TEA ROOMS
Barwon Security

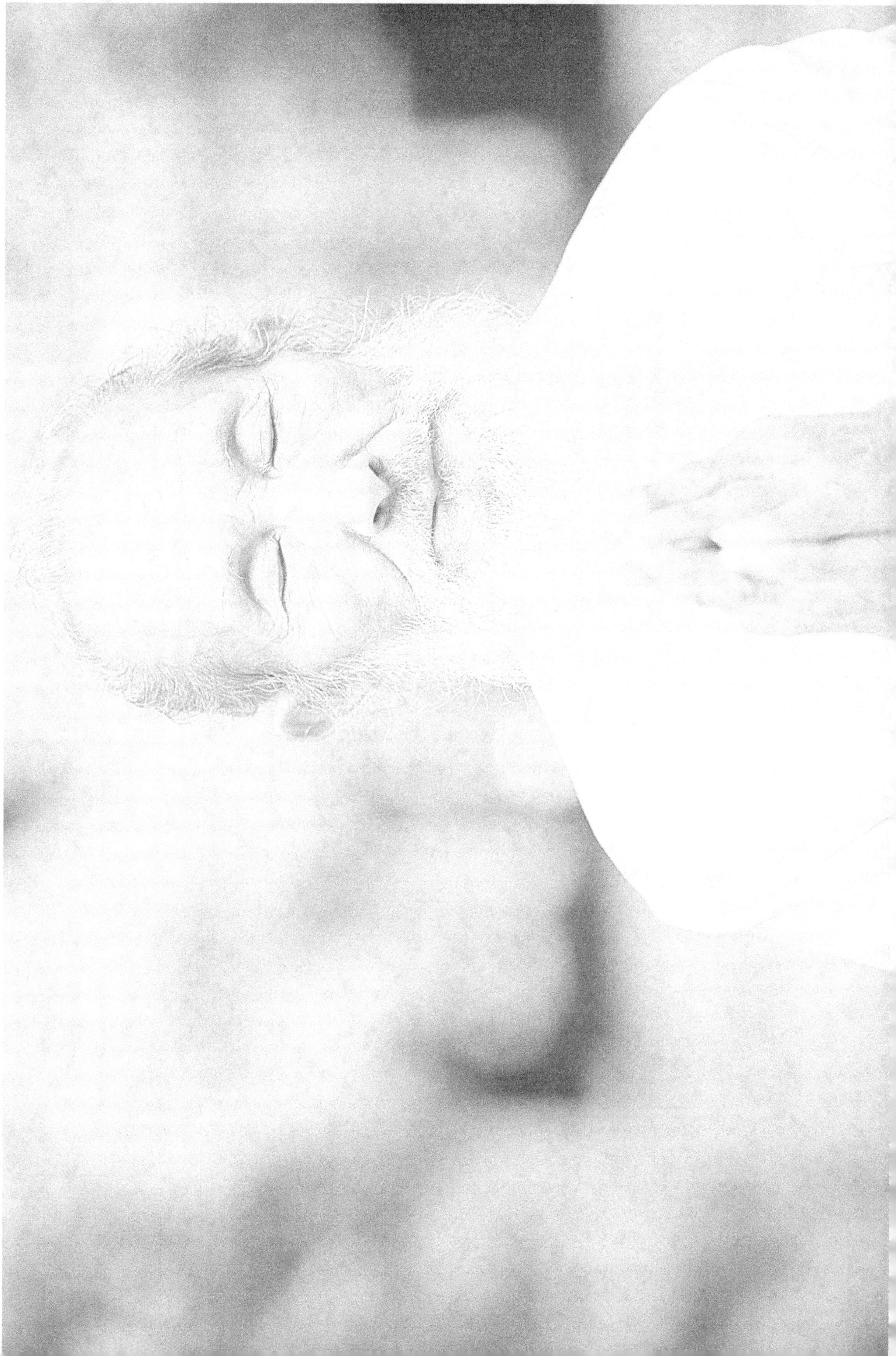

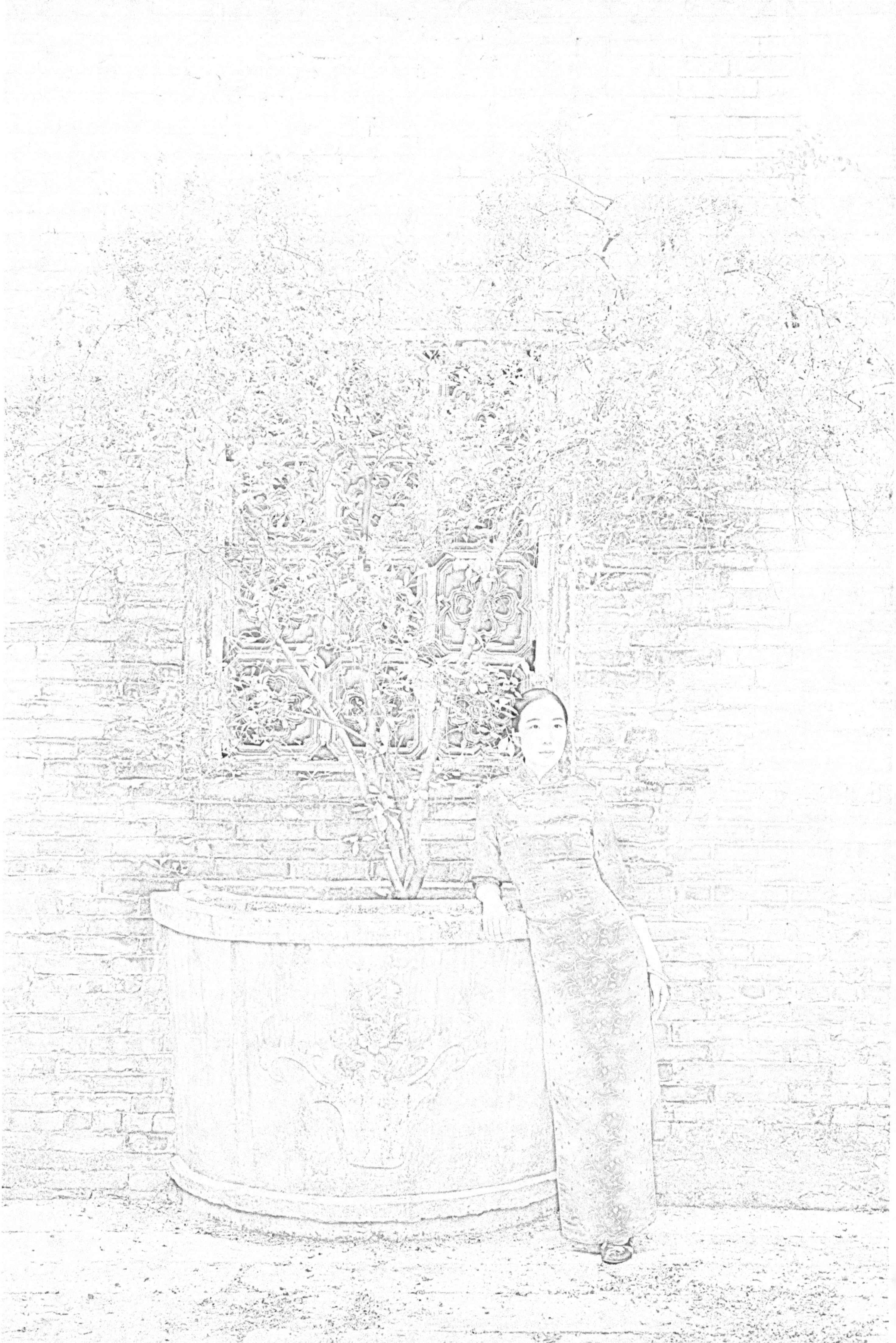

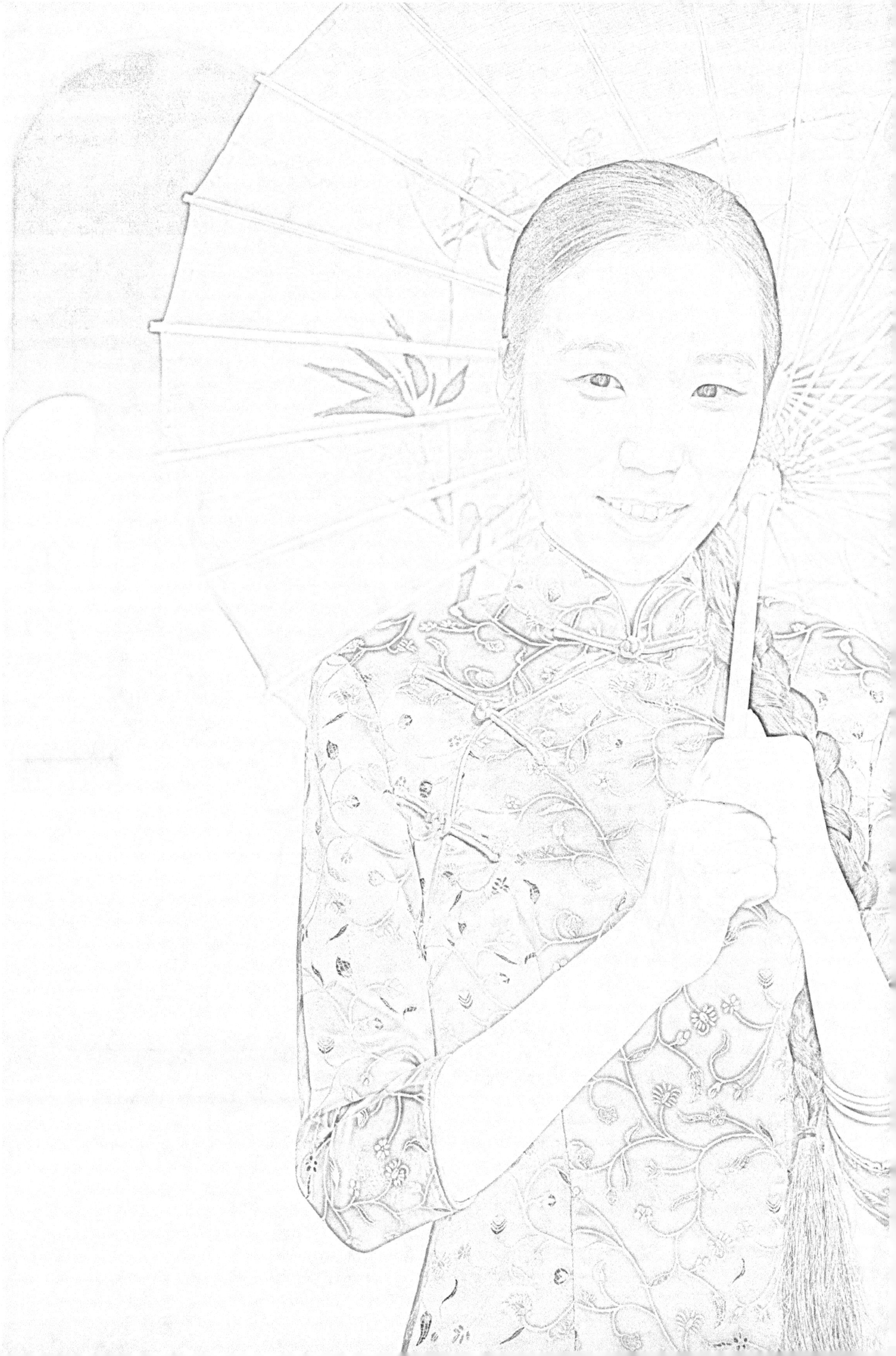

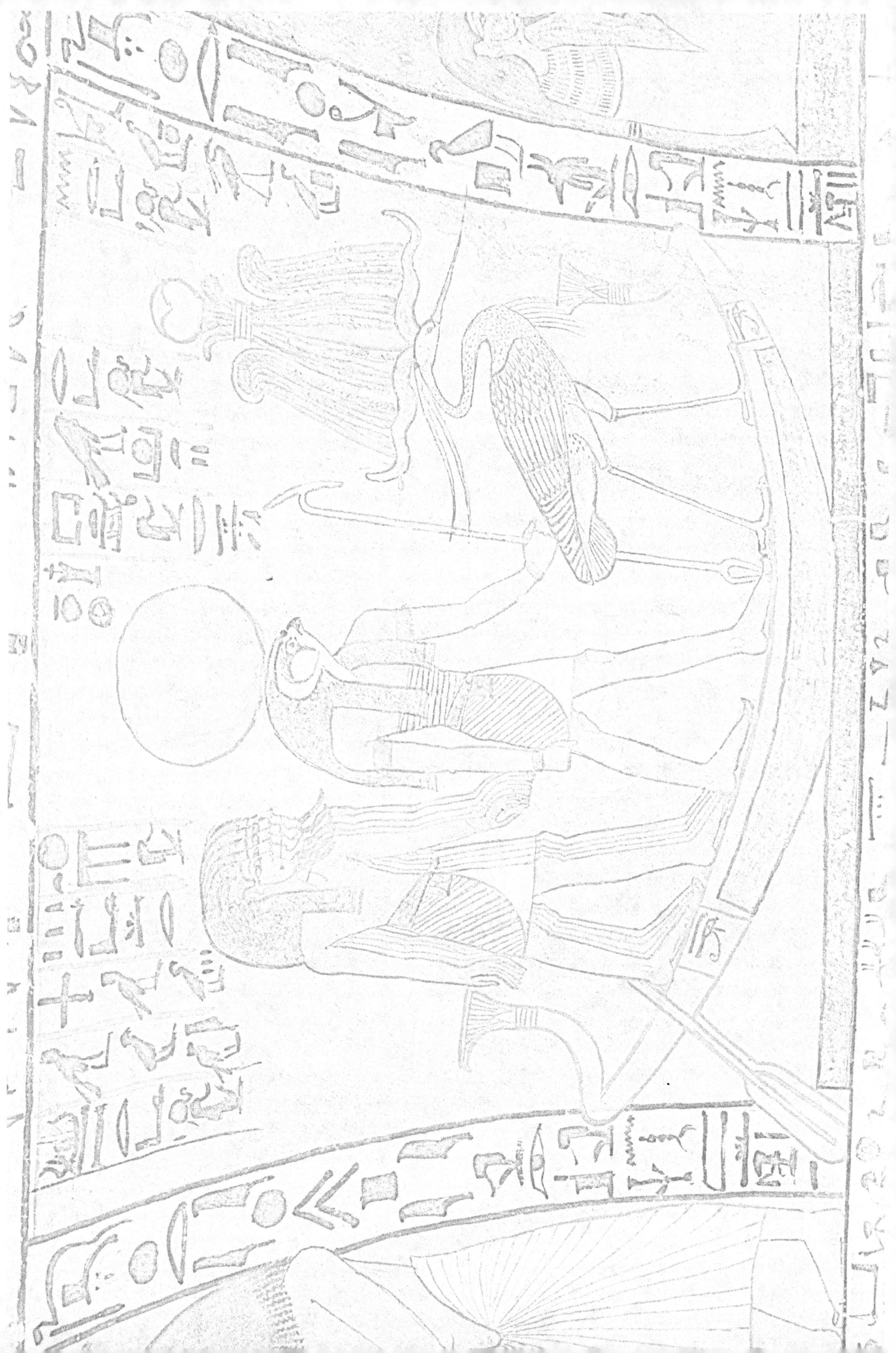

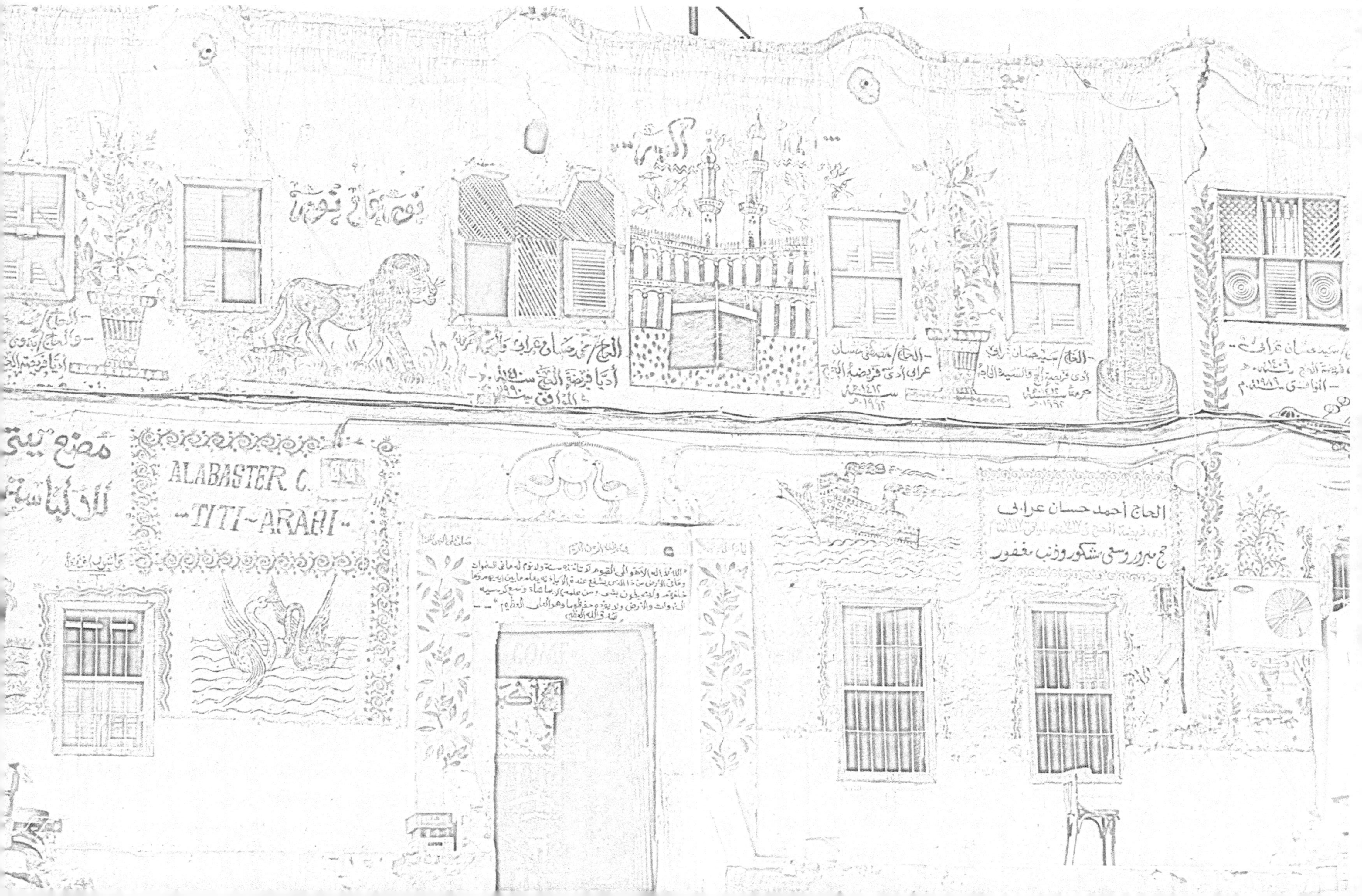
ALABASTER C.
-TITI-ARABI-
الحاج أحمد حسان عرابى
حج مبرور وسعى مشكور وذنب مغفور

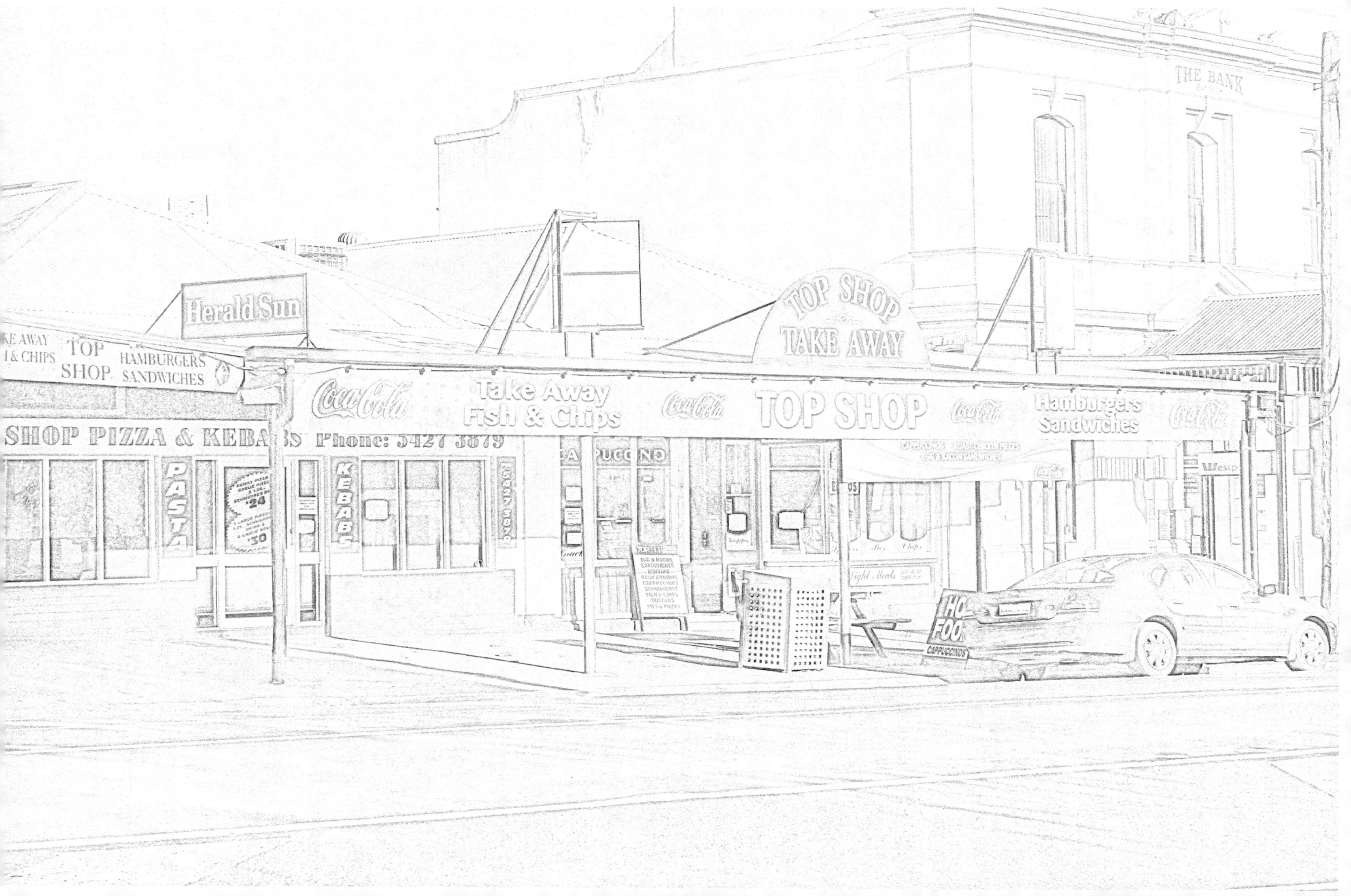
THE BANK
Herald Sun
TOP SHOP
TAKE AWAY
KE AWAY
I & CHIPS
TOP SHOP
HAMBURGERS
SANDWICHES
SHOP PIZZA & KEBABS
Phone: 5427 3879
Coca-Cola
Take Away
Fish & Chips
TOP SHOP
Hamburgers
Sandwiches
PASTA
KEBABS
5427 3879
$24
$30
CAPPUCCINO
Westp
HO
FOO
CAPPUCCINOS
EGG & BACON SANDWICHES
CAPPUCCINOS
SANDWICHES
FISH & CHIPS
BURGERS
PIES & PIZZAS

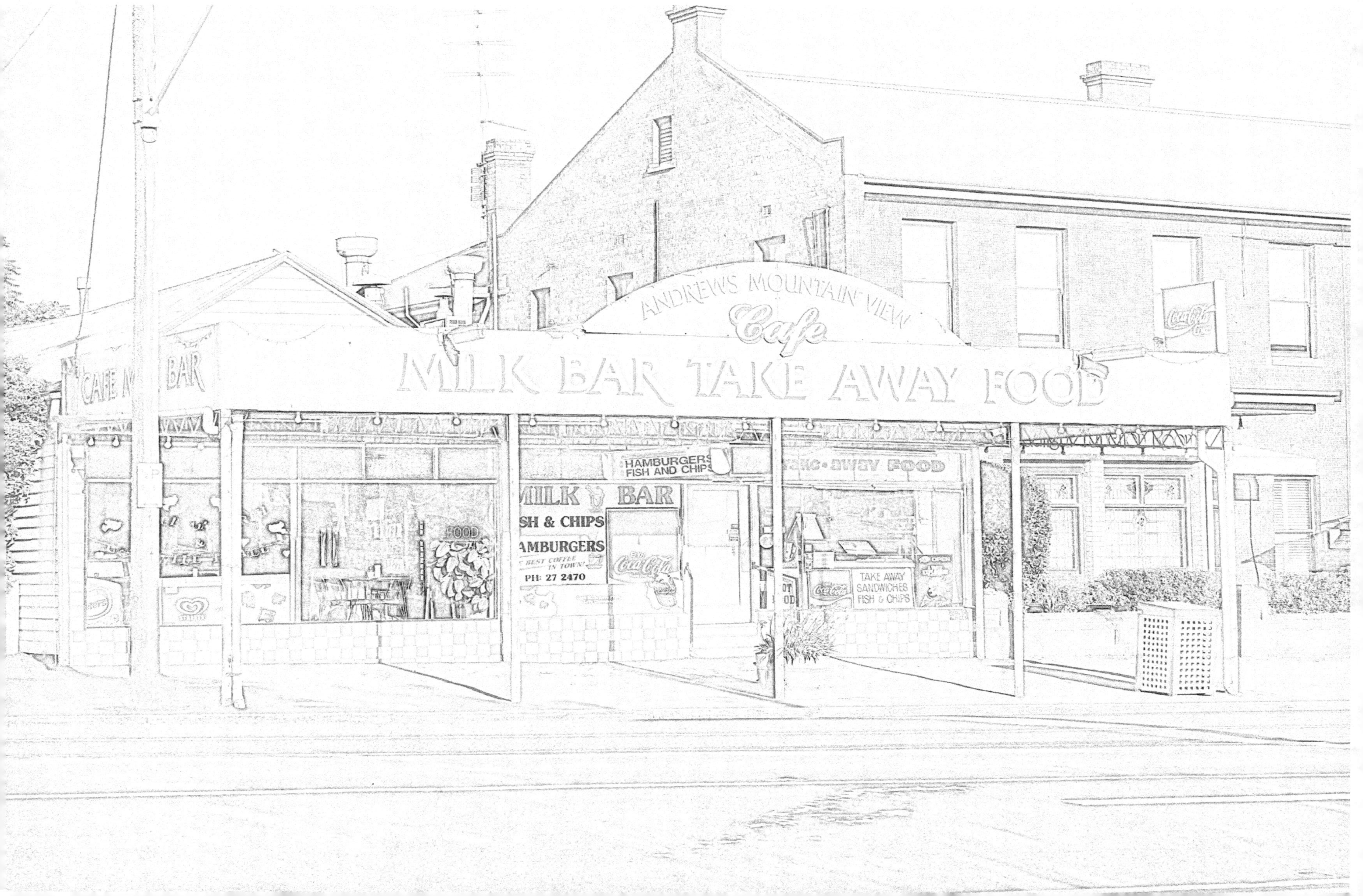
ANDREWS MOUNTAIN VIEW
Cafe
MILK BAR TAKE AWAY FOOD
CAFE
BAR
HAMBURGERS
FISH AND CHIPS
MILK BAR
SH & CHIPS
AMBURGERS
PH: 27 2470
FOOD
TAKE AWAY
SANDWICHES
FISH & CHIPS

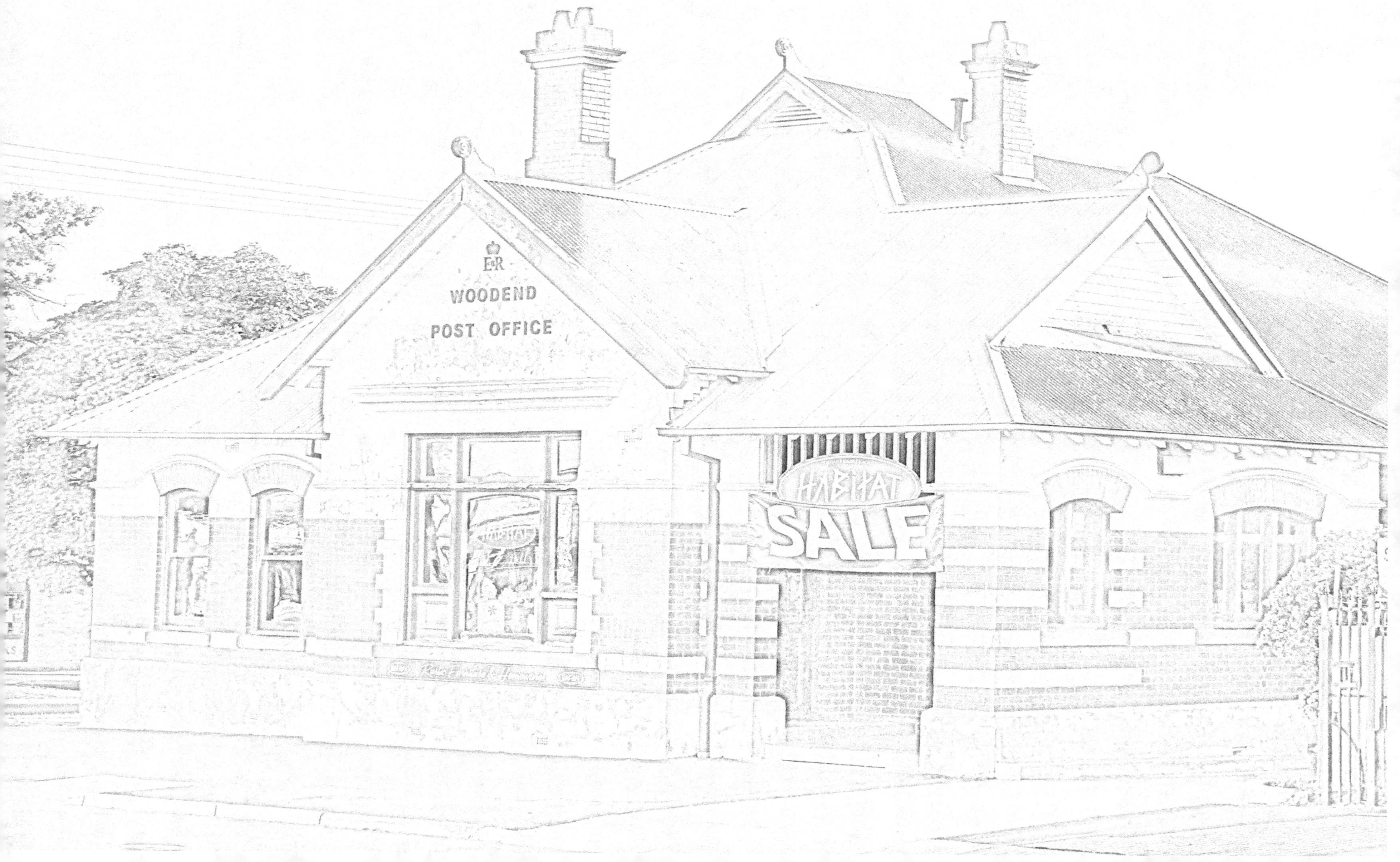
E R
WOODEND
POST OFFICE
HABITAT
SALE

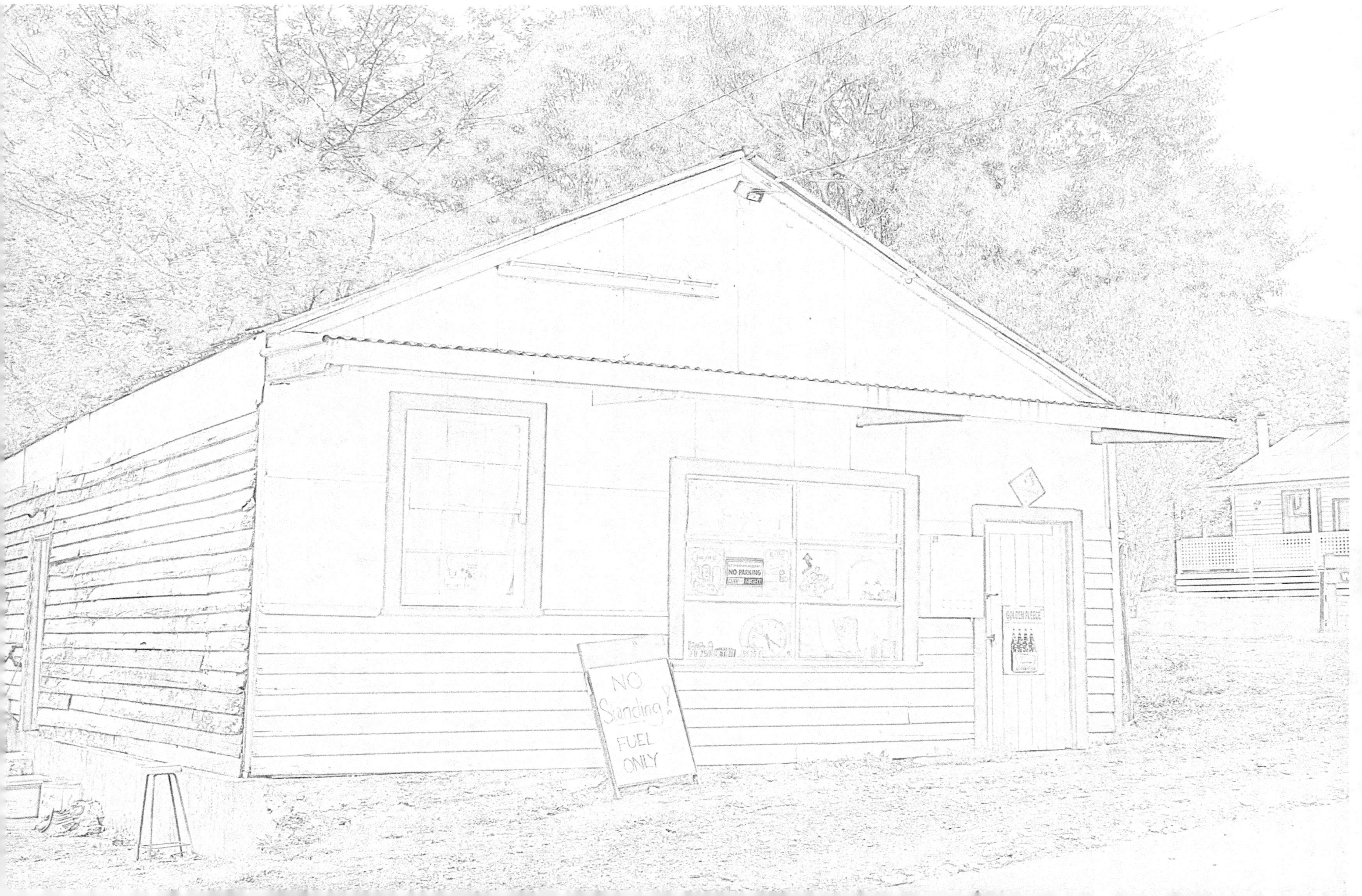
NO PARKING
DAY NIGHT
NO Standing!
FUEL ONLY
GOLDEN FLEECE

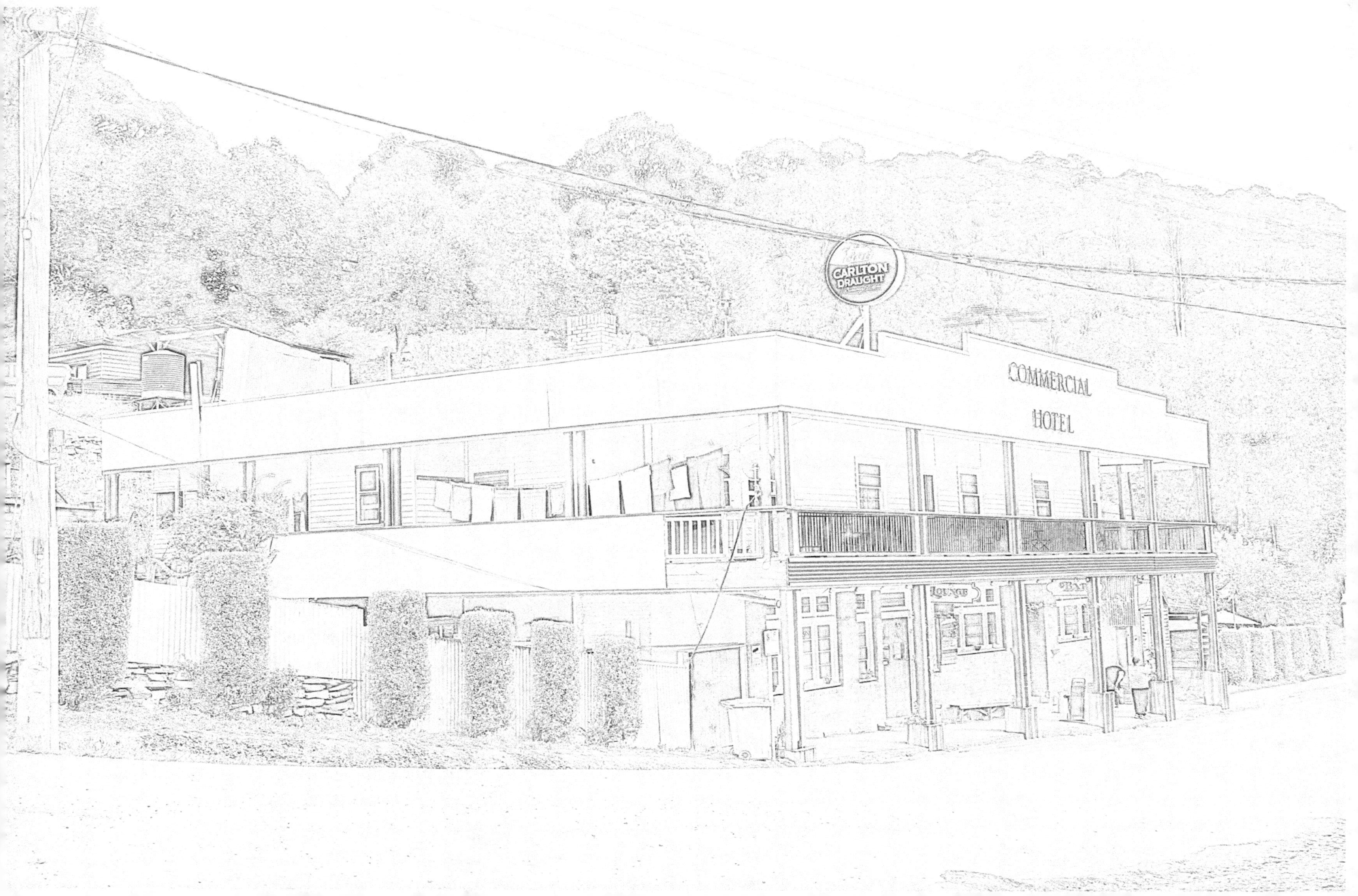
CARLTON DRAUGHT
COMMERCIAL
HOTEL
LOUNGE

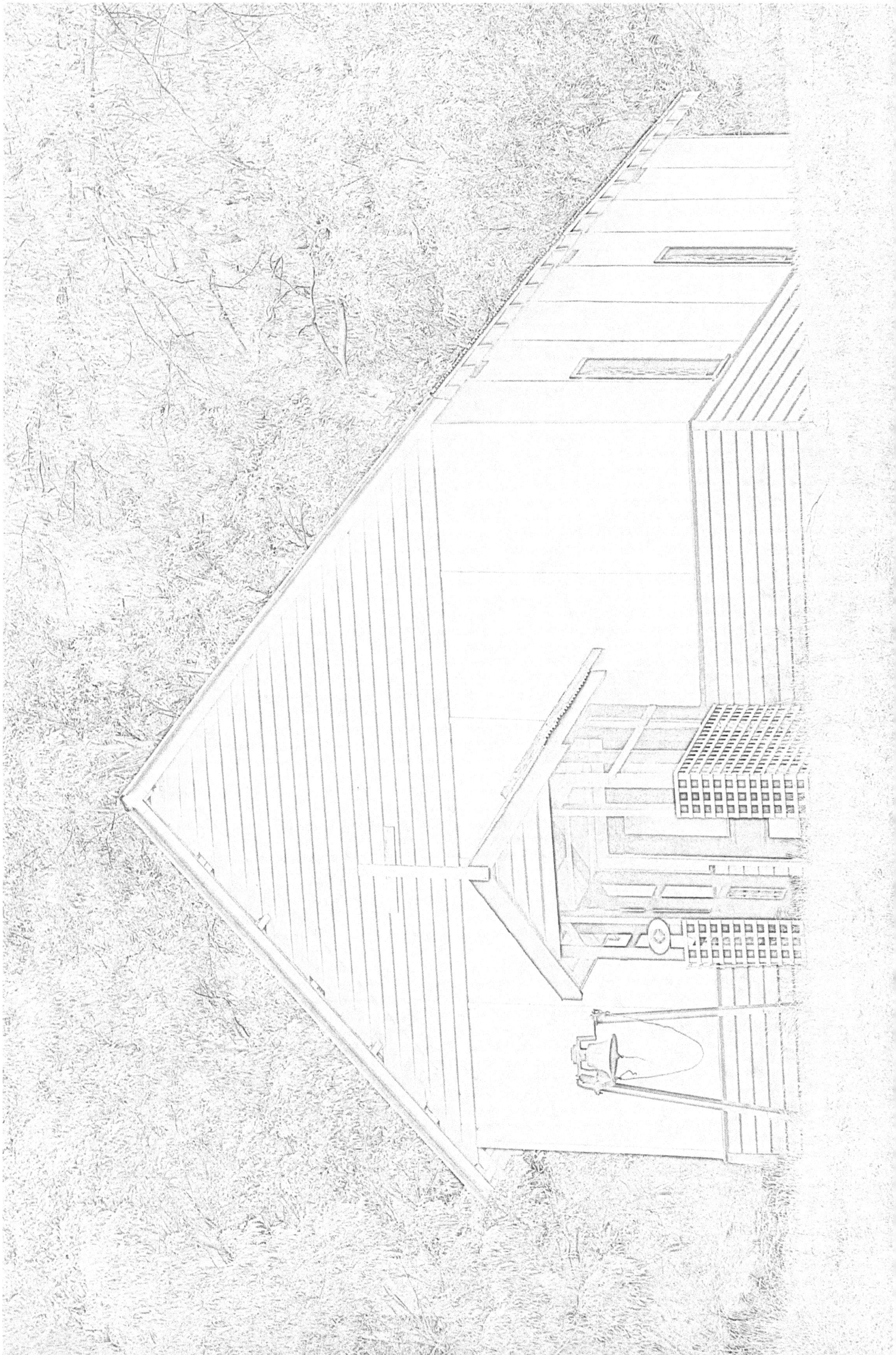

Wesburn Baptist Church
SUNDAY SERVICES
Morning Worship: 10.30 am
Evening Worship: 5.00 pm
NO SERVICE
TONIGHT

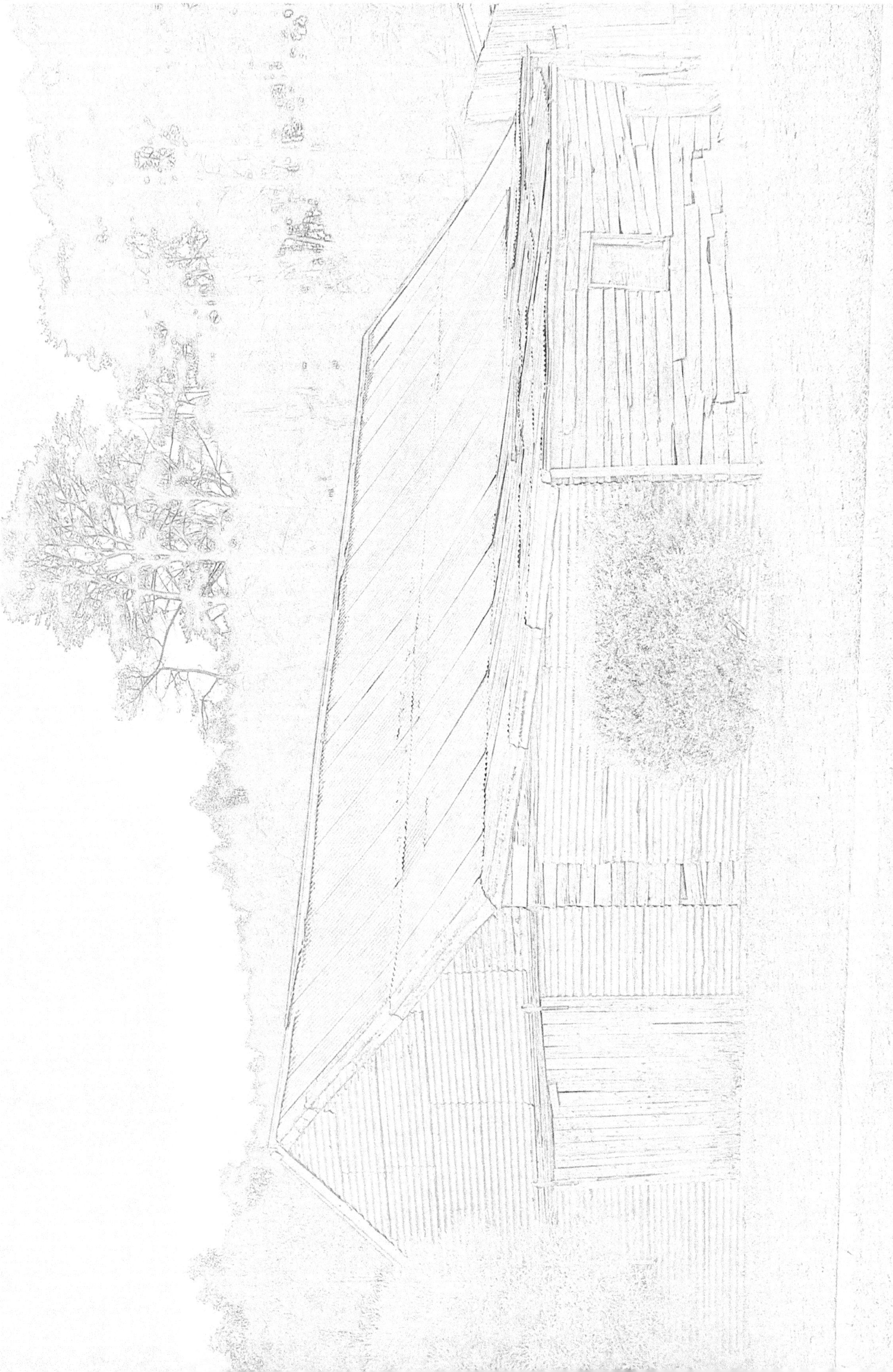

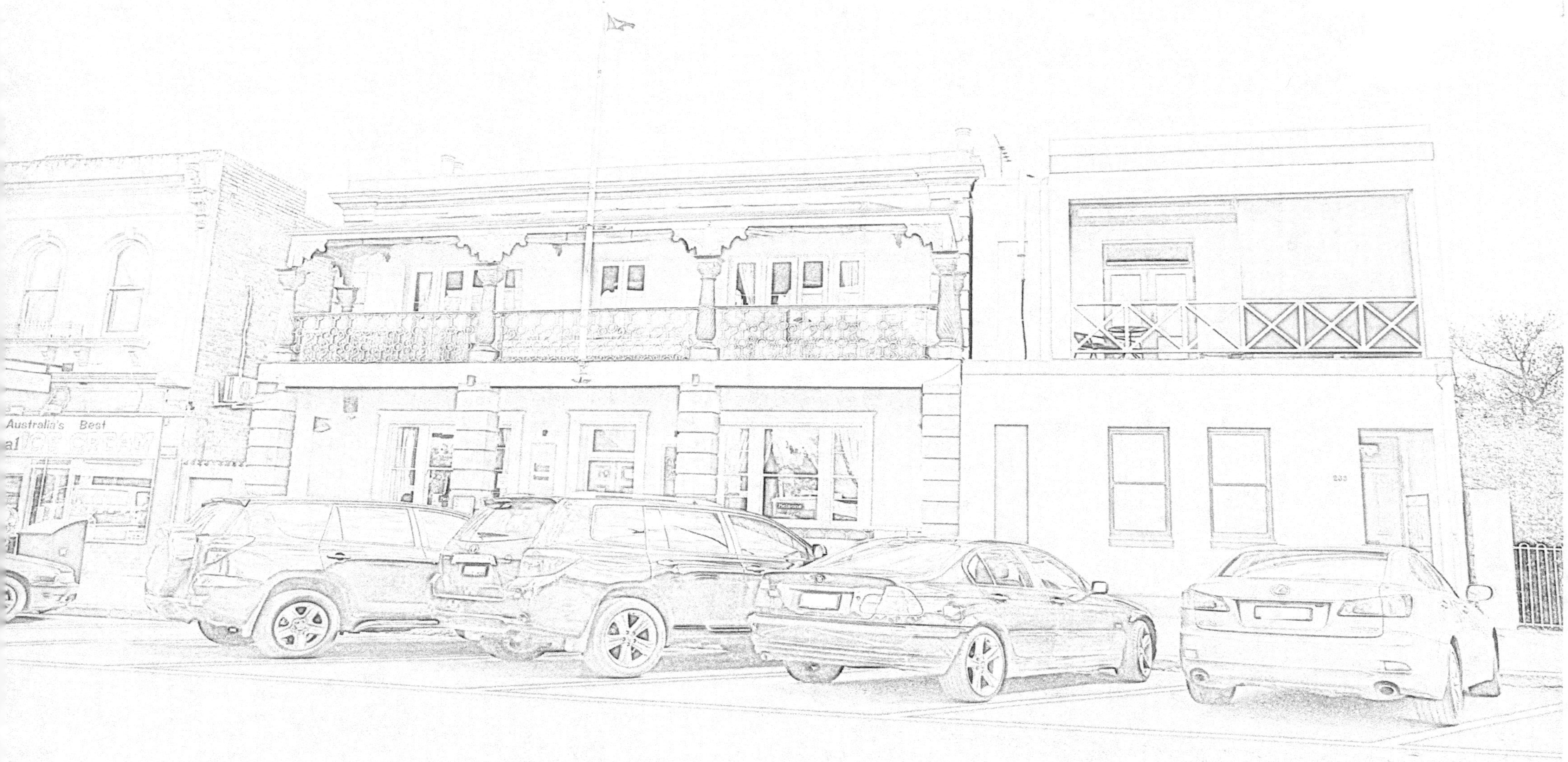
Australia's Best
ICE CREAM
233

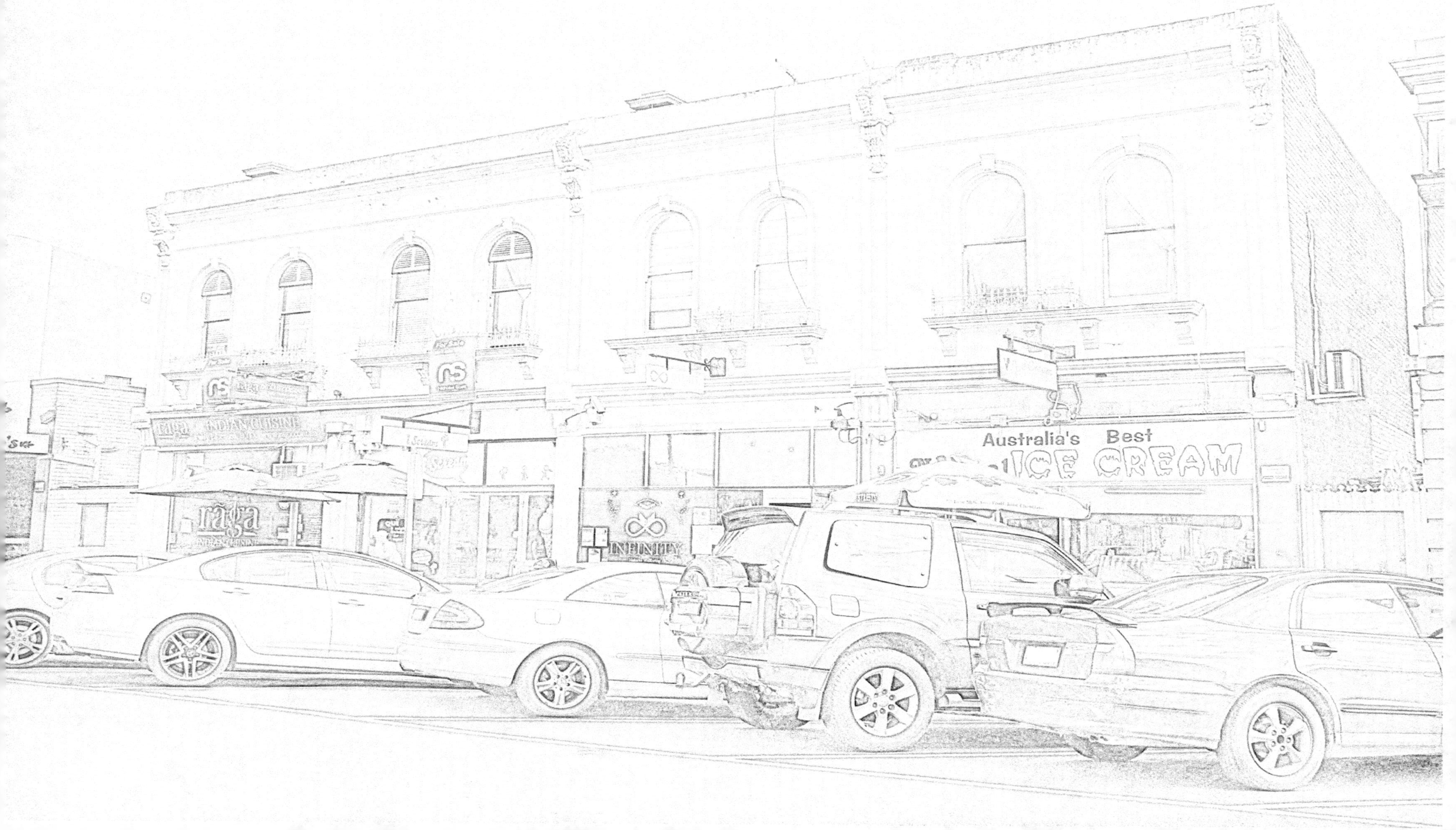
Australia's Best ICE CREAM
raga INDIAN CUISINE
raga
INFINITY

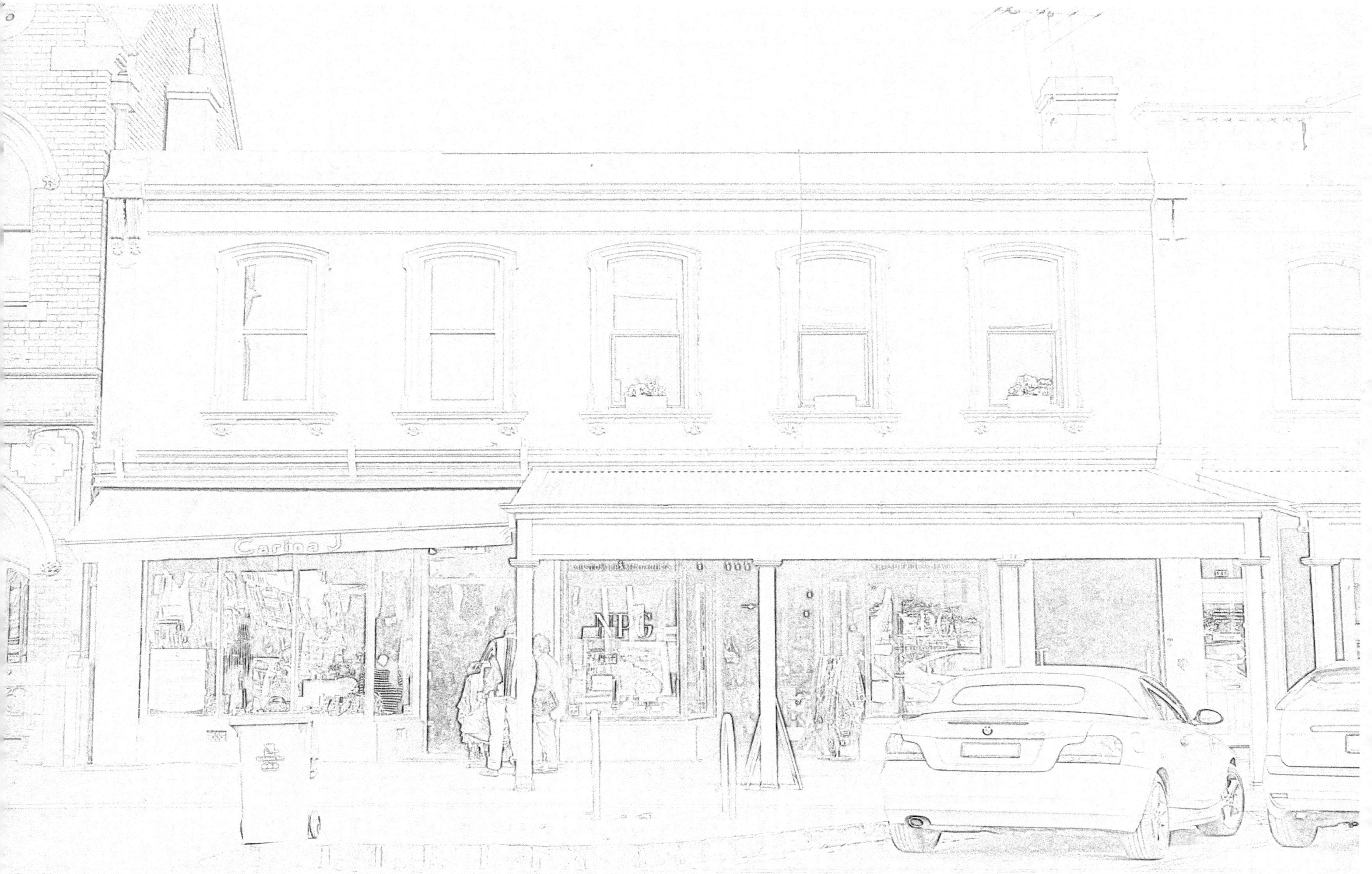
Carina J
NPG

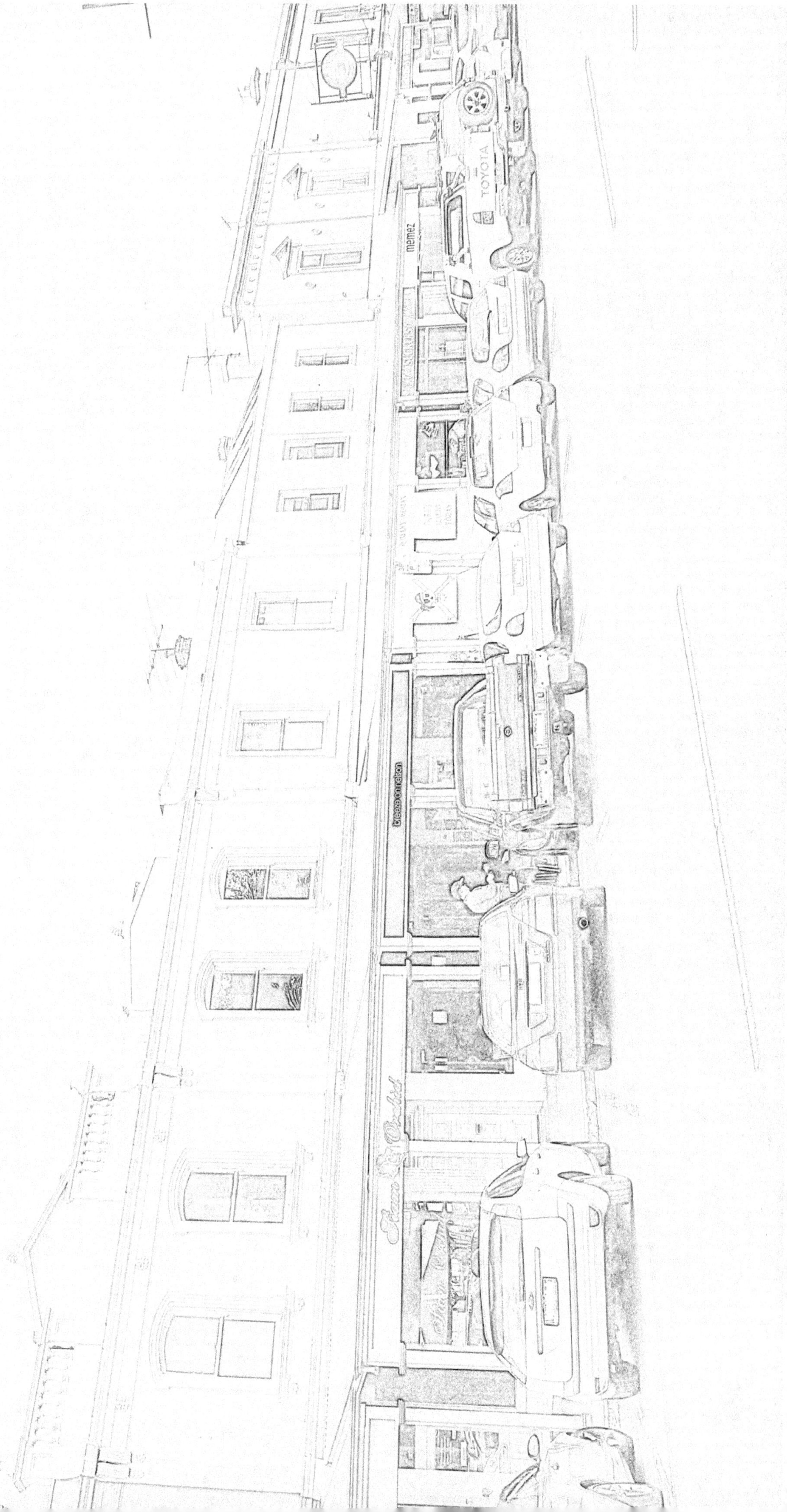
TOYOTA
memez

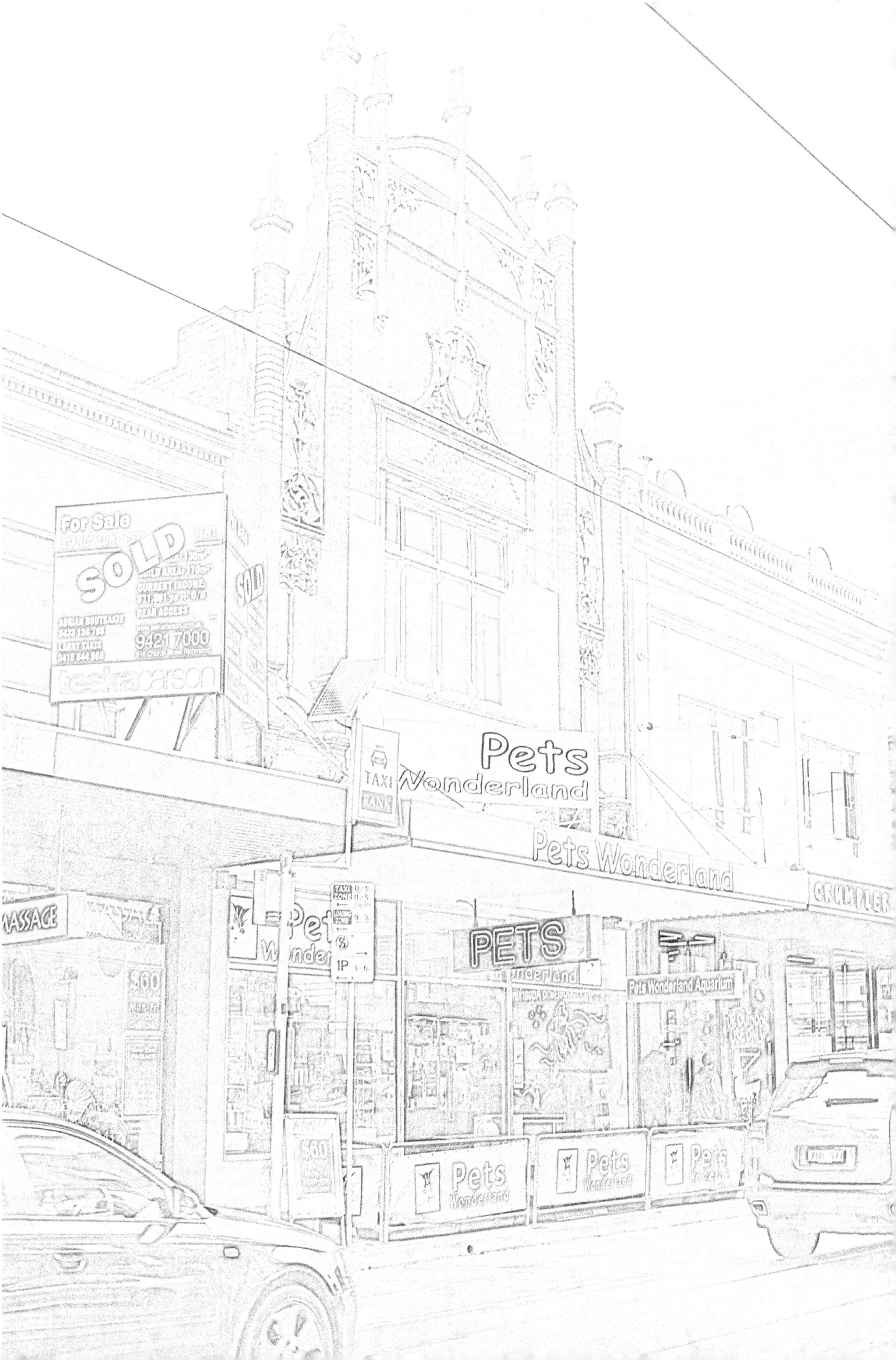
For Sale
SOLD
9421 7000
teskacarson
SOLD
TAXI
RANK
Pets
Wonderland
Pets Wonderland
CRUMPLER
MASSAGE
$60
PETS
Pets Wonderland Aquarium
1P
$60
Pets
Wonderland
Pets
Wonderland
Pets

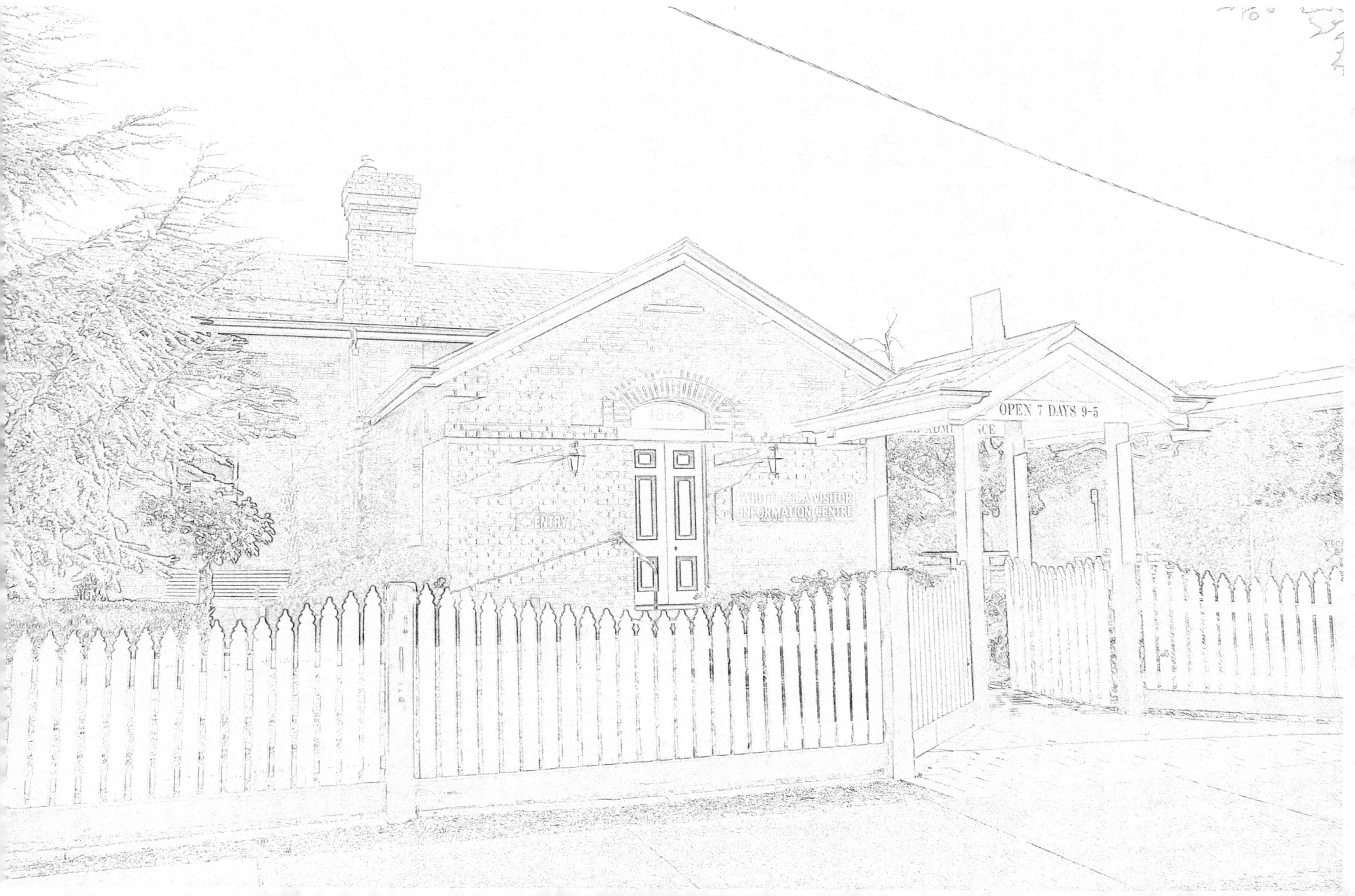
OPEN 7 DAYS 9-5
WHITTLESEA VISITOR
INFORMATION CENTRE
ENTRY
1864

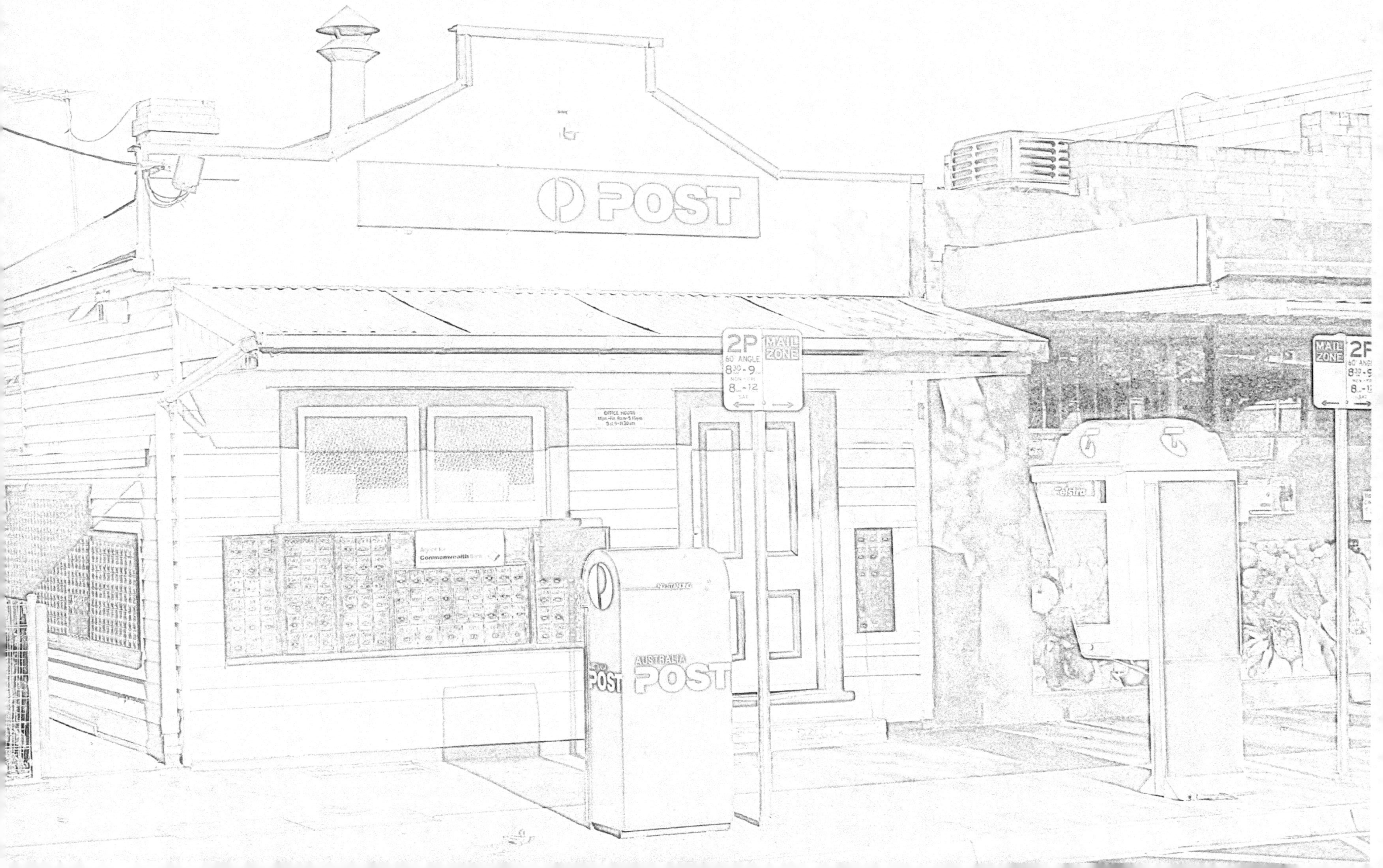
POST
2P
60° ANGLE
MAIL ZONE
AUSTRALIA POST
Commonwealth Bank

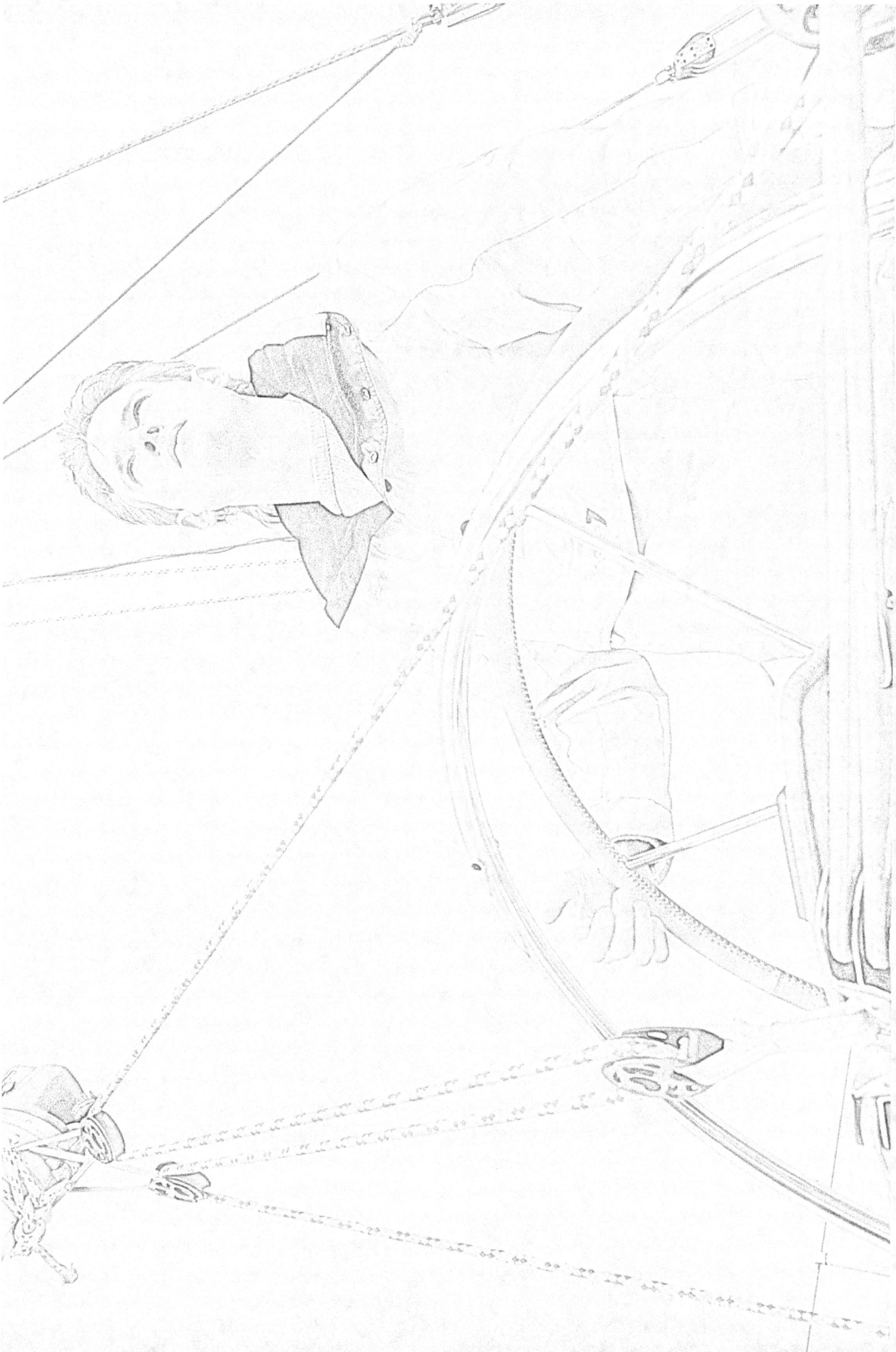

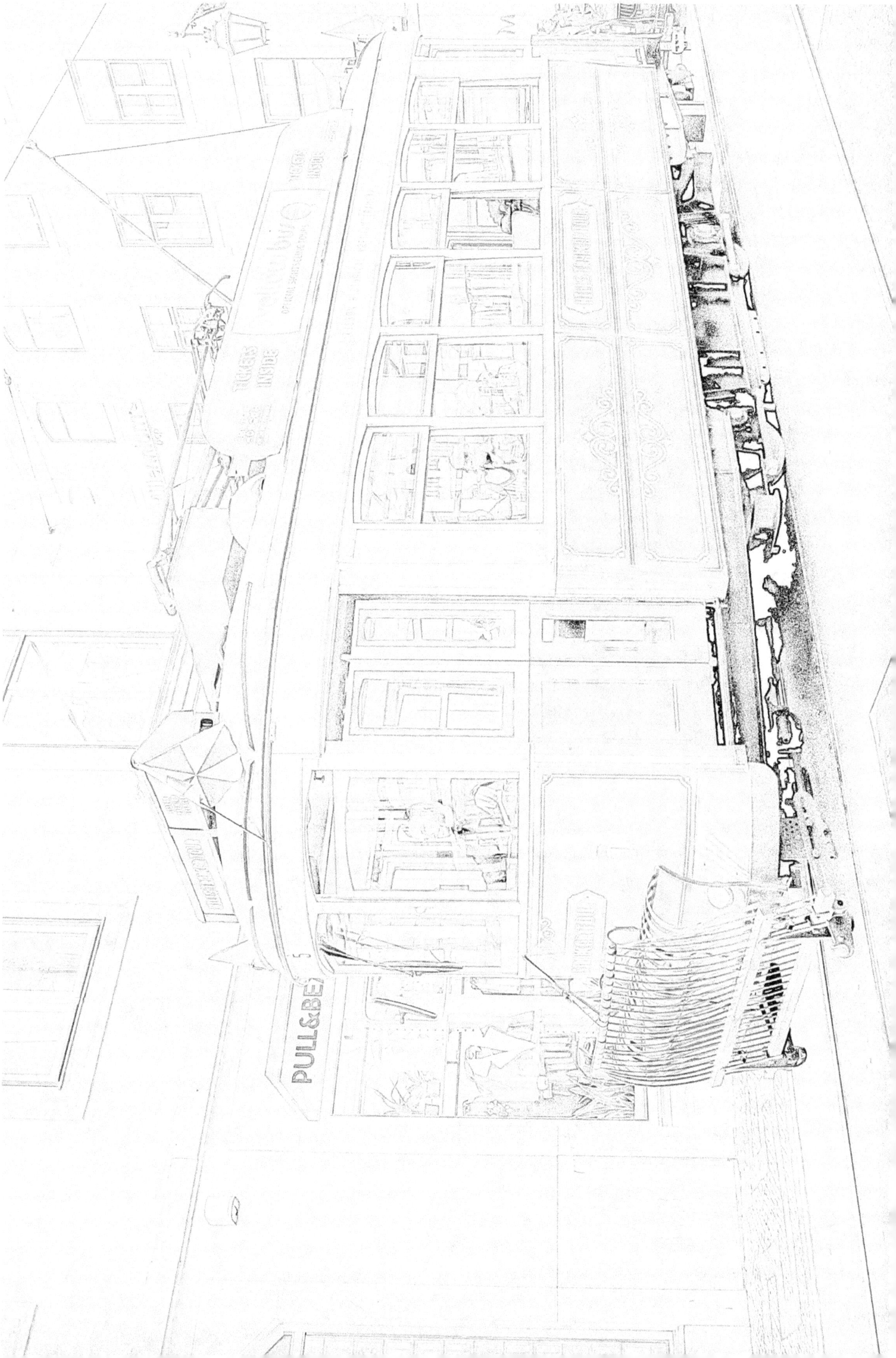
PULL&BE

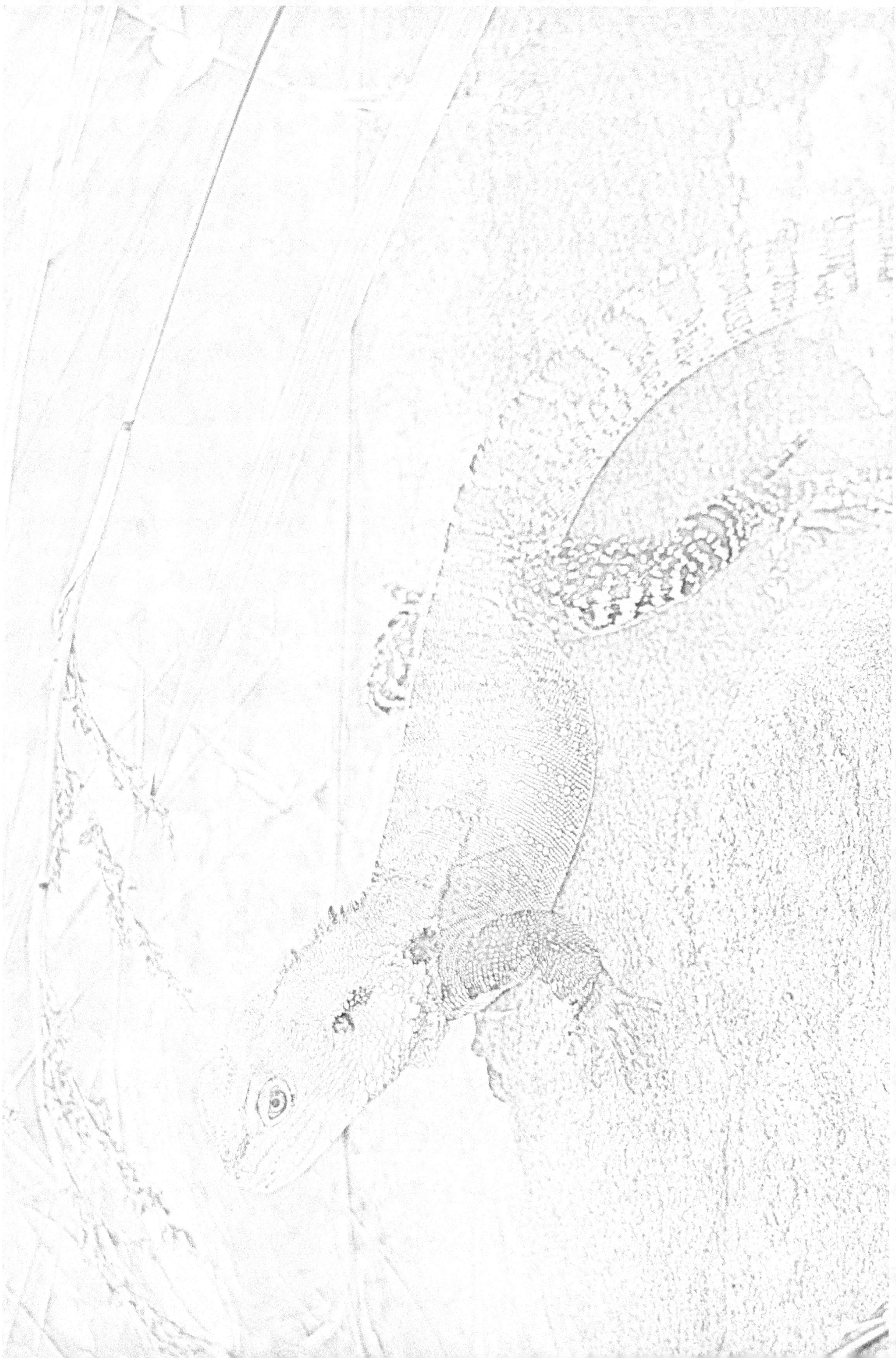

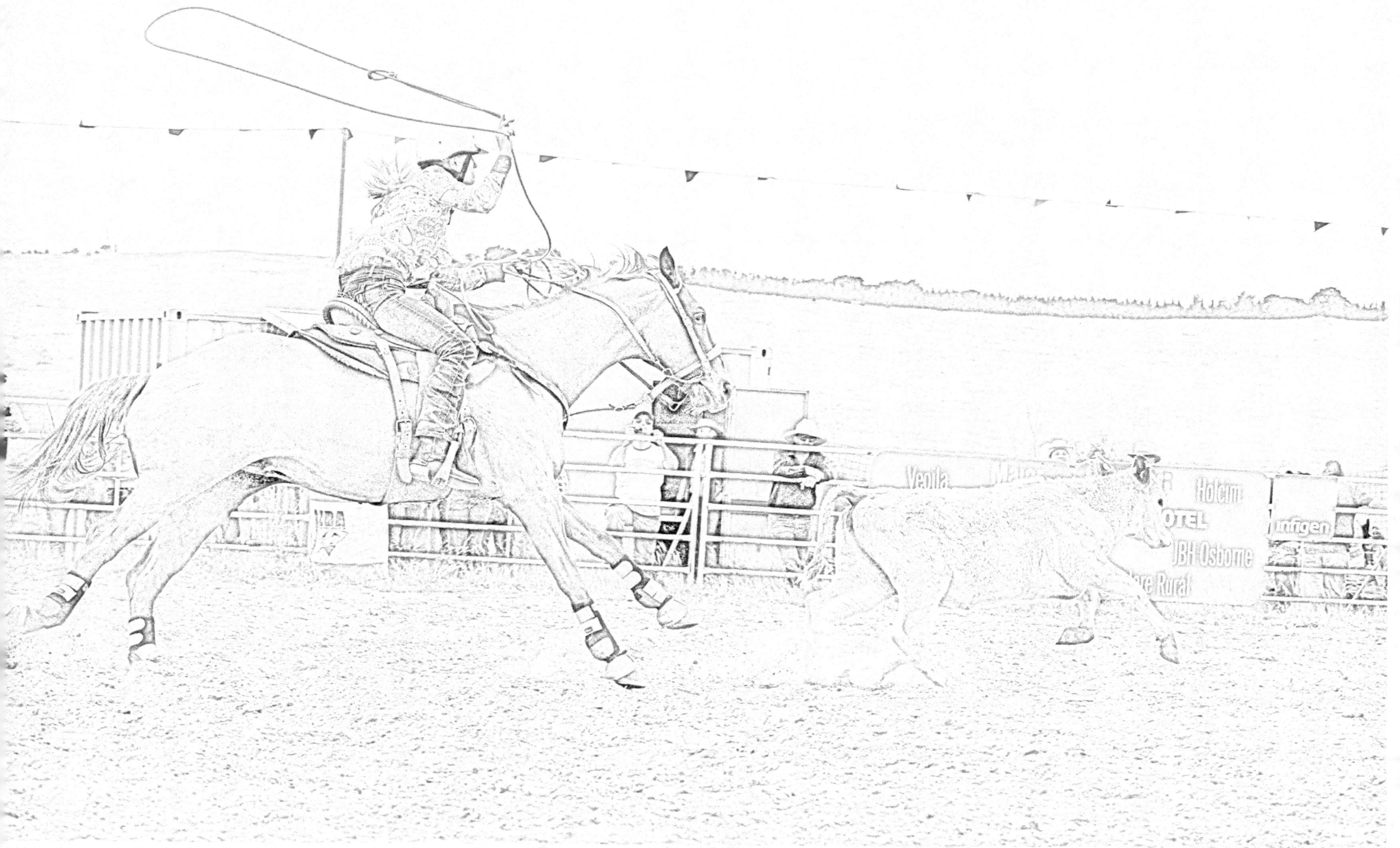
Holcim
JBH Osborne

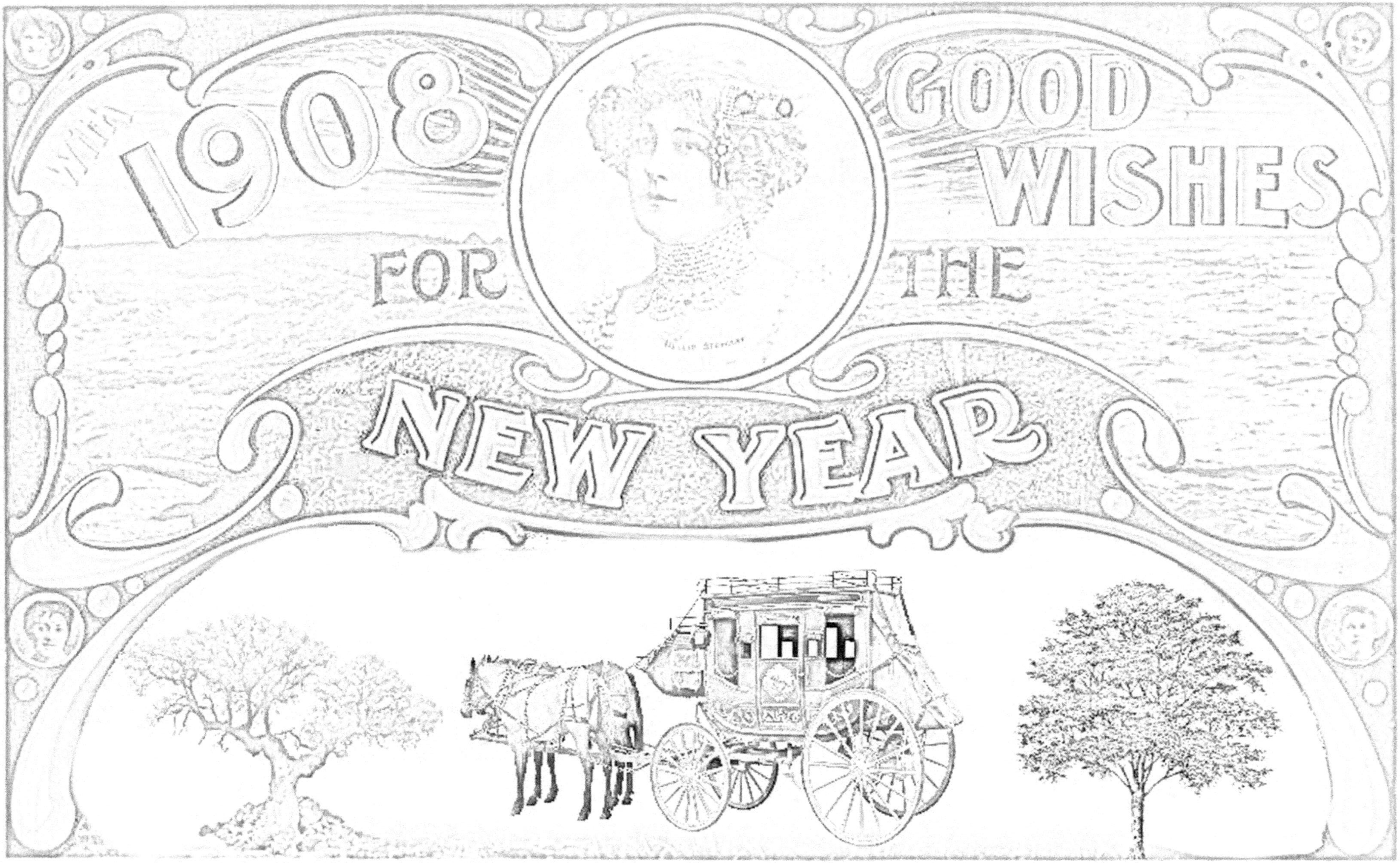
WITH 1908 GOOD WISHES
FOR THE
NEW YEAR

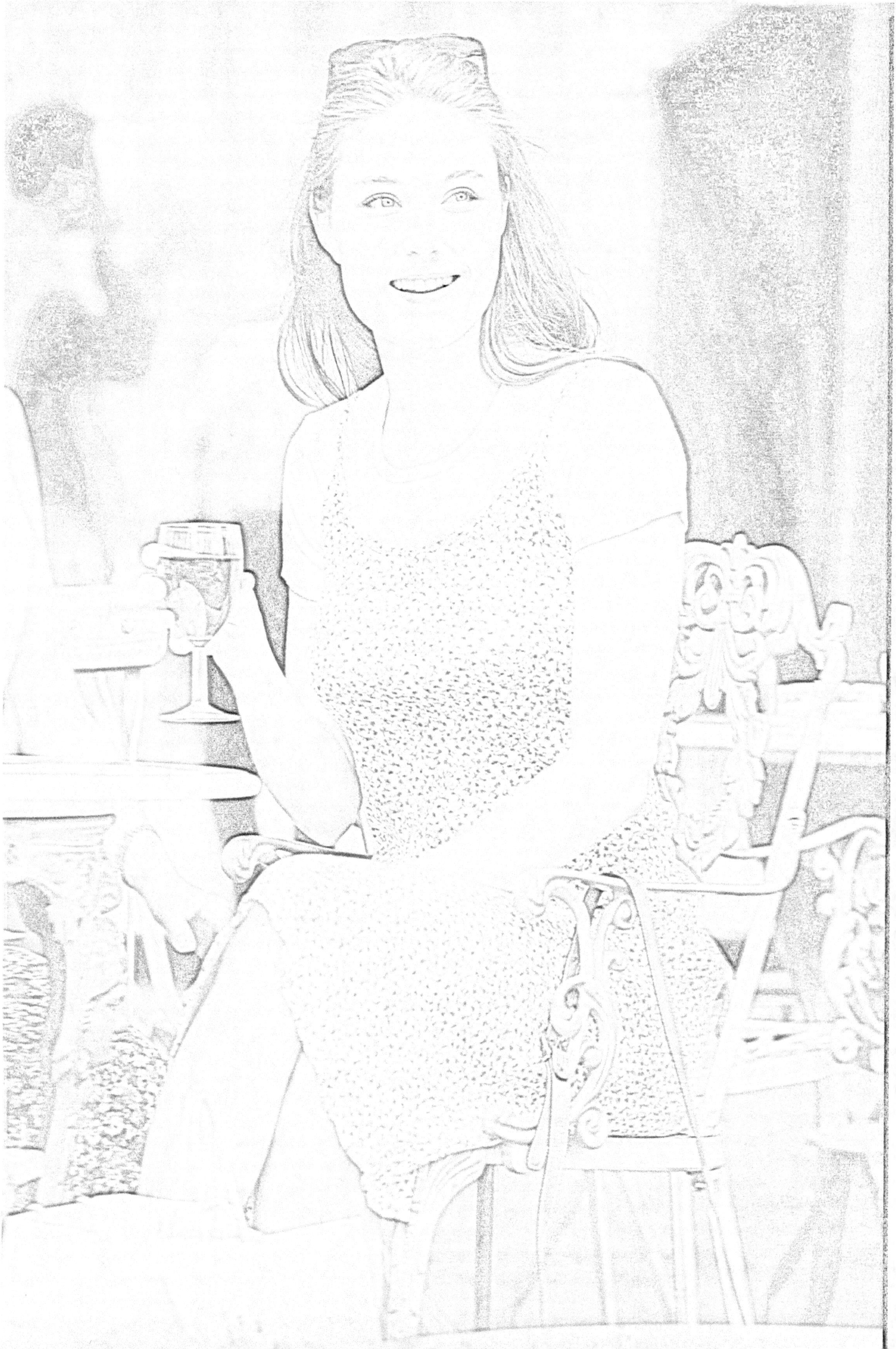

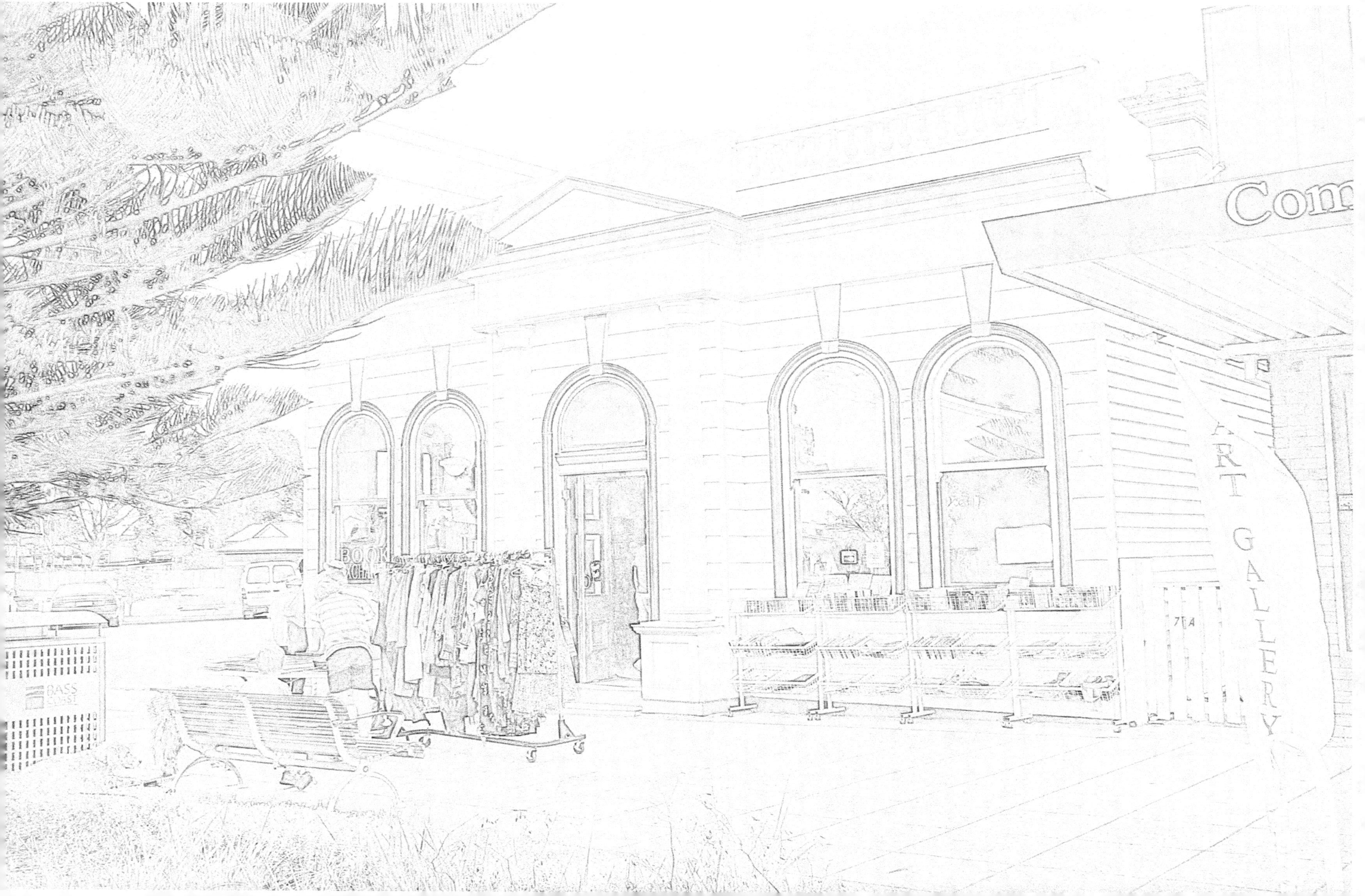
Com
ART GALLERY
BASS COAST

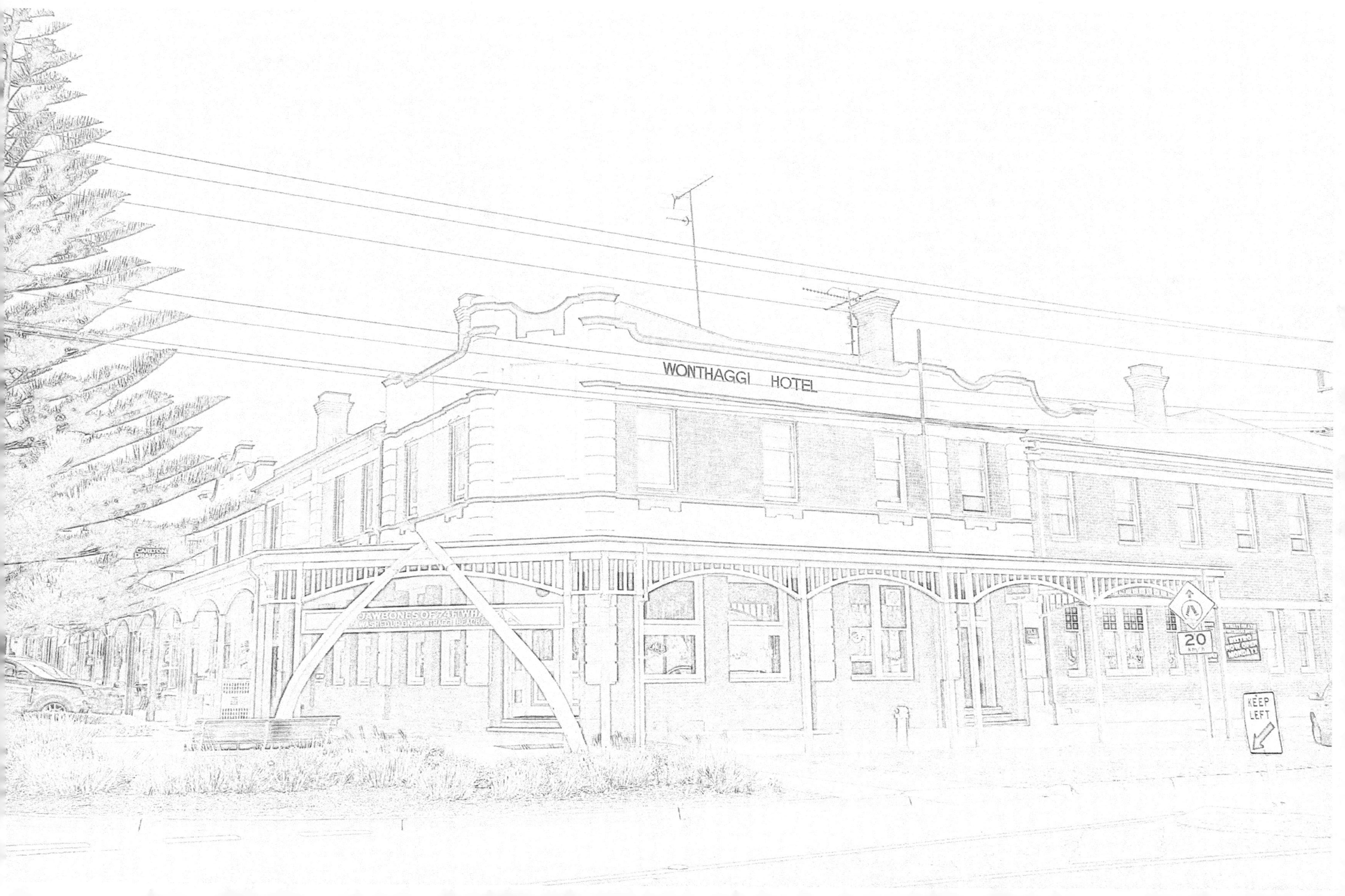
WONTHAGGI HOTEL
20
KEEP LEFT

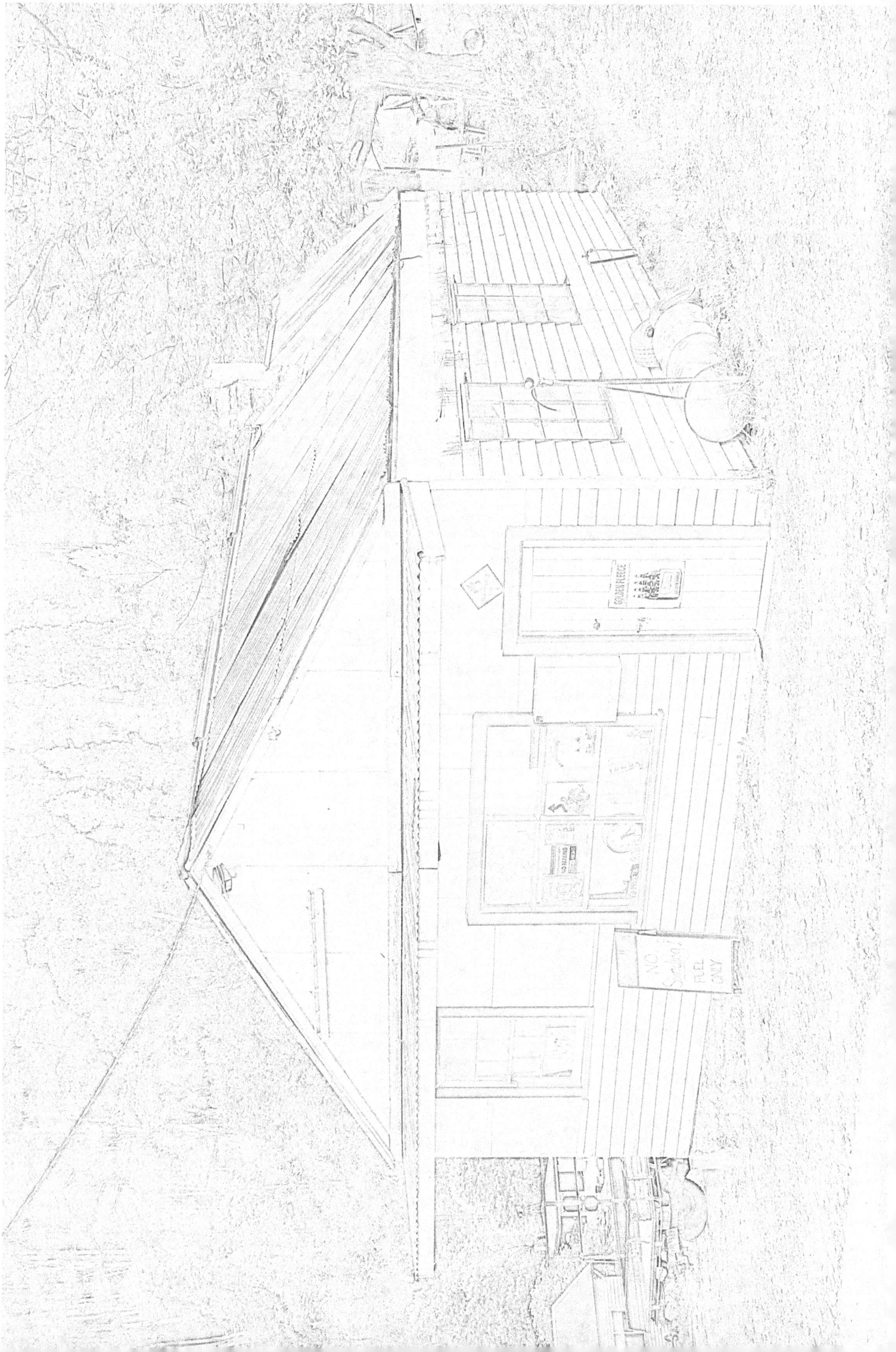
GOLDEN FLEECE
NO
FUEL ONLY

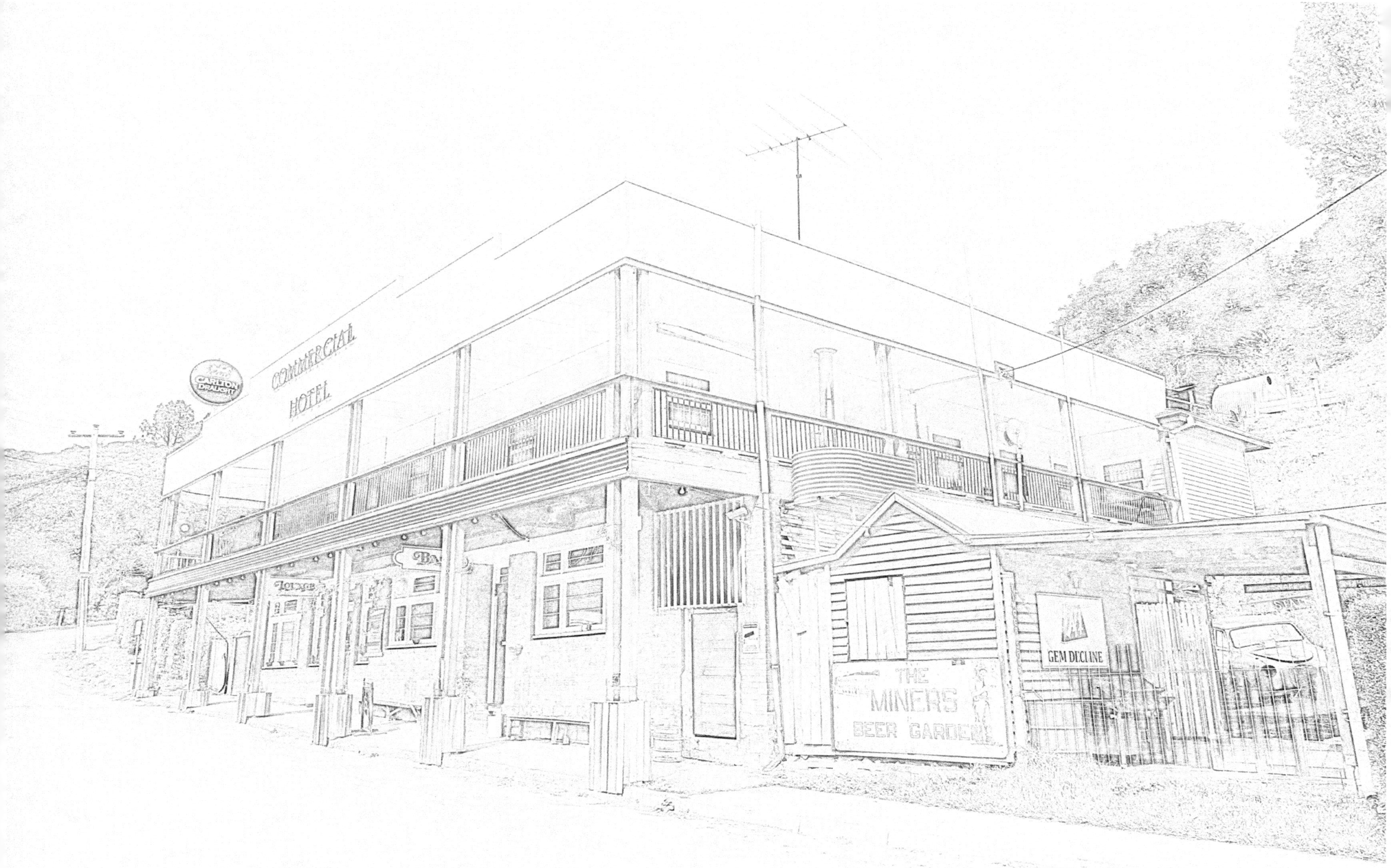
CARLTON DRAUGHT
COMMERCIAL
HOTEL
LOUNGE
THE
MINERS
BEER GARDEN
GEM DECLINE

www.ingramcontent.com/pod-product-compliance
Lightning Source LLC
Chambersburg PA
CBHW081056180526
45170CB00005B/1781
* 9 7 8 0 3 5 9 8 6 3 3 2 7 *